Progression in Primary ICT

Richard Bennett
Andrew Hamill
& Tony Pickford

David Fulton Publishers

David Fulton Publishers Ltd
2 Park Square
Milton Park
Abingdon
Oxford OX14 4RN

www.fultonpublishers.co.uk

First published in Great Britain in 2007 by David Fulton Publishers

10 9 8 7 6 5 4 3 2 1

David Fulton Publishers is an imprint of the Taylor & Francis Group, an informa business.

British Library Cataloguing in Publication Data
A catalogue record for this book is available from the British Library.

ISBN-10: 1-84312-308-8
ISBN-13: 978-1-84312-308-8

Typeset by Servis Filmsetting Ltd, Longsight, Manchester
Printed and bound in Great Britain

Contents

Acknowledgements

The authors would like to thank Julie Cross and children from Class 2 of Willow Wood Community Nursery and Infant School for sharing their ideas for using digital video with the authors.

Introduction

This series of books, Teaching ICT through the Primary Curriculum, is based on the belief that the integration of primary ICT into the curriculum is of benefit to children's development in both ICT and the other subjects through the Foundation stage, key stage 1 and key stage 2. By incorporating some of the powerful ICT tools described in the projects, the quality of your teaching and children's learning will improve. Similarly, by contextualising the children's ICT experience in meaningful projects you will enhance children's ICT capability.

This book is the core text for the series that includes books on learning ICT in the arts, the humanities, science, mathematics and English.

We start this book with a discussion of the rationale behind our approach, which is based on our own experience of teaching and mentoring. Chapter 2 is a discussion of progression in ICT as well as an overview of the projects in the series. Issues relating to planning for ICT are examined in Chapter 3. In Chapter 4 the assessment of children's ICT capability is discussed and in Chapter 5 the organisation and management of ICT resources in the primary school are examined. In Chapter 6 we muse on some of the probable developments in technology that might impact on teaching and learning in the not-too-distant future.

We have developed this series to meet the needs of primary practitioners with whom we have engaged in hundreds of hours of conversation in ICT training suites and classrooms. It is also based on our extensive experience of primary classroom teaching and the development and delivery of courses in primary ICT for serving teachers and those in training.

We believe this book will contribute to the initial and continuing professional development of all primary teachers.

Throughout, we keep in mind the ways you can help your children learn effectively:

- let them know why an activity is important for them

- show them how to access information that can help them

- relate the activity to their experience

- make sure they are ready and motivated to learn

- help them overcome inhibitions or negative attitudes to learning.

But more important than the wealth of ideas in the subject books and the issues discussed in this book is the personal justification for the role of ICT in learning that you will construct as you engage with the ideas presented here. It is your personal beliefs and enthusiasm that make your teaching effective.

In each of the projects in this series we identify real reasons for using ICT. In this book we share our reasoning behind the structure, content and approaches we describe, to sustain you in justifying your use of ICT, now and during the next evolution of ICT.

This book, the subject books and the accompanying CD-ROMs include useful resources and dynamic sources of information that will help you stay abreast of developments. Appropriate software and ways to use it are described in detail in each project.

The required ICT standards for teachers are embedded in this series in a way that makes the work fun. Although we cannot hope to have addressed every facet of your professional experience, we have pooled our considerable knowledge of primary practice to provide useful information for both new and experienced ICT teachers.

As primary practitioners we are all motivated by the children we teach and our desire to see each one make progress. This series aims to help you challenge your children in ways that make sense to them, and to equip you with the knowledge and understanding to be confident in your planning, organisation and teaching.

If we were to ask what single thing gets in the way of professional development in ICT, the reply would probably be 'time'. To help you focus your time on those aspects of professional development that are most important to you, we have included fact cards in the subject books. These give a very quick overview of each project. Each project has a section that takes you through a task, step by step, one possible way. Many projects also have example files in a variety of formats on the accompanying CD-ROMs.

In summary, this book aims to provide you with background knowledge about why ICT should be incorporated into your teaching, ideas for how to use ICT and information to help ensure your children make progress in the development of their ICT capabilities through interesting and meaningful contexts.

Quick-start your professional development

- List all the things that are getting in the way of your professional development in ICT.
- Identify the ones you can do something about.
- Think of a strategy for overcoming the ones within your control.
- Identify who you need to talk to about the others.

CHAPTER 1

A rationale for teaching ICT

The main purpose of this chapter is to explore beliefs about the way we think ICT can and should be taught. It is always possible to avoid giving a personal rationale for what and how we teach by referring to the National Curriculum and schemes of work. While we must be aware of the requirements outlined in national and local policy documents, a personal commitment to the content of our teaching, and the approaches that we adopt, will translate into an integrity in our classroom practice. To that end, what children learn and how they learn are examined in more detail in this chapter.

Before we start, however, it is worth pointing out two aspects of ICT that we are *not* aiming to cover in this book. The first is a wider justification for ICT in the curriculum. Those arguments have been very well rehearsed by others (Loveless and Dore 2002; Sharp *et al.* 2002; Kennewell *et al.* 2000; Ager 2000). The central, if not the core, position of ICT in the primary curriculum has become established, and so we focus on the values and purposes of integrating and embedding ICT in the ways we have described in the projects contained in the other titles in this series.

Nor do we dwell in this series on those aspects of ICT that concern its use solely as a professional tool, if it does not make a positive contribution to the development of ICT capability in children. That is not to belittle its usefulness as a tool for the teaching, learning and wider professional duties of a teacher; it is because we wish to scrutinise, in particular, those aspects of ICT use which help children to develop their knowledge and understanding of ICT.

If we were to represent the totality of a teacher's professional use of ICT diagrammatically it might look like Figure 1.1.

Some ICT use by teachers is to help children achieve subject learning through activities that use existing ICT knowledge and skills to discover information or

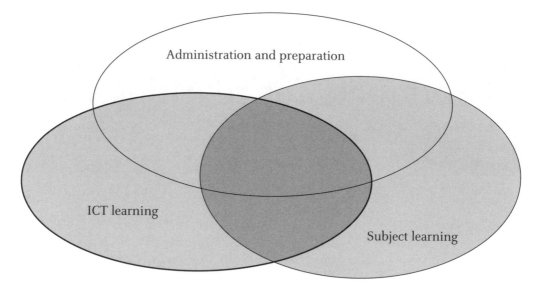

Figure 1.1 Teachers' professional use of ICT

communicate findings. Similarly, some is for administration and preparation, to present teaching and to record children's learning. Finally, some is specifically aimed at developing children's ICT capability, and at helping them to become more knowledgeable about the subject and more proficient users. It is this last use of ICT that concerns us, in particular the intersection between ICT and subject learning. Selinger (2001) makes a distinction between teaching *about* ICT and teaching *through* ICT. This series focuses on reaching ICT capability through other subjects.

In each of the projects in the series we put forward pragmatic and instrumental justifications for teaching ICT in the 'Why teach this?' sections. There we discuss some of the reasoning behind the projects and why we advocate teaching ICT through the primary subjects.

In particular we discuss:

⊙ learning and how children learn – lessons from andragogy and ICT, and learner-centred education, and ICT and multimodal learning

⊙ the curriculum and what children learn – the overloaded primary curriculum; the integration of domains of knowledge; the processes of data-handling; creativity; enquiry and ICT; ICT and independent choices; an index of curricular integration; and the planning of symbiotic outcomes.

Learning and how children learn

Much of our understanding of how children learn has been influenced by theorists and researchers of the nineteenth and twentieth centuries; in particular the constructivist theories of Piaget and Vygotsky, interpreted by Bruner and Donaldson. Those working in early years settings continue to be inspired by the principles of Montessori, Froebel and others. None of these key theorists, however, experienced for themselves what happens when young learners are given access to the technologies which surround us in education today. The reason why their names are familiar is for the enduring resonance that their ideas have with our observations of children learning in our classrooms and the ease with which we can interpret their principles and apply them to new ideas.

Montessori, for example, believed in educating the senses through the manipulation of materials. She developed activities specifically to engage and develop children's senses. She also sought to devise materials that would ensure that children were in control of their learning, encouraging them to investigate and explore. It is not hard to imagine that Montessori would have been keen to exploit the potential of ICT to allow children to explore and investigate making their own decisions. Active learning and real decision-making has long been recognised as a powerful factor in effective learning. Through controlling events in a computer model (see *Learning ICT with Maths* project 8) or creating art work (see *Arts* projects 2 and 5) or exploring the living world (see *Science* projects 2 and 8 and *Humanities* project 7), children are able to develop their skills and understanding as they make real decisions.

Papert, inspired by Piaget, was the first of a new wave of pioneers who sought to develop ICT tools that would harness the emergent understanding of how children learn by building constructive feedback into software that responds to young learners' choices. From the initial versions of turtle LOGO (see *Maths* project 7) to the construction of Microworlds (see *Arts* project 8), the LOGO environment has been developed to mirror the building of understanding through assimilation of ideas which fit within current understanding, and accommodation of ideas that require a restructuring of our knowledge, as described by Piaget. Children developing a LOGO project are cast in the role of teacher; their errors are not their own, but misunderstanding on the part of the computer. When the software indicates that it does not know how to carry out a command, the child is faced with analysing the problem. When a turtle moves in an unexpected way the child has to think again and try to understand the way that the computer has acted on the commands given. Although the total immersion in LOGO projects has only really been achieved in some experimental settings, the provisional nature of ICT tools has enabled child-centred exploration of ideas in the LOGO spirit to be realised using a range of software only dreamed of when LOGO was first conceived. When using vector drawing software (see *Arts* project 3), presentation software (*Science* project 7) or digital video (*Arts* project 10; *Humanities* project 9; *English* project 8), children are able to develop their own ideas, imagine possibilities and learn from the effects of their decisions.

Child-centred education has received some bad press over the years but has recently undergone a revival with the publication of *Every Child Matters* (DfES 2004) and the focus on individualised learning. The principle is alive in personalised learning, made possible by ICT which enables learning to be tailored to the needs of individual learners and provides instant feedback based on the choices they have made. Because of the way that ICT can put powerful tools within the reach of young children and make them more independent learners at an early age, it is possible that there are lessons for primary ICT learning that can be learned from andragogy, the study of how adults learn. Indeed, it has been argued that without a shift to more learner-centred education we will be unable to keep up with the pace of technological change, as today's children will ultimately need to be able to teach themselves. If they wait for a teacher to interpret each new development in technology during their lives they will be unable to participate effectively in society.

Lessons from andragogy and ICT, and learner-centred education

The term 'andragogy' was originally used to describe the study of how adults learn. It has developed into a term that emphasises learner-centred education (Knowles 1990) for learners of all ages and is particularly pertinent to views of the development of ICT capability and current calls towards more personalised learning (e.g. DfES 2004).

In this section we will consider how principles outlined in an andragogic model are particularly suited to ICT learning.

An andragogic model of learning, as we discussed at the outset, suggests that five key strategies are important for effective learning to occur:

1. Let the learners know why the activity is important for them to learn.

2. Show the learners how to access information to help them.

3. Relate the activity to the learners' experience.

4. Make sure the learners are ready and motivated to learn.

5. Help them overcome inhibitions or attitudes to learning.

Although it is argued that the relating of activities to young learners' experience may be more difficult, as they have fewer of these on which they can draw, the type of autonomy that we are trying to encourage – to make independent choices in their uses of ICT – will be promoted through these more learner-centred strategies. Also the type of learning that ICT makes possible, by providing access to a vast range of information, individual support through on-line help and individual feedback on the effects of choices, as children explore simulations and develop their own ideas, makes the andragogic model particularly applicable to ICT learning.

Why the activity is important

By designing activities in each of the projects that make use of ICT for a purpose, in a context that makes sense to children, the ICT learning necessary to undertake the tasks is justified. Many of the projects (e.g. *Learning ICT in the Arts* projects 5, 8 and 9) also engage the children in creative activities that will lead to them not only solving problems but also finding and creating problems of their own as they strive to make things happen according to their plans and designs. These types of 'child-created' problems can be the most engaging, because it is important for the children to make their picture or design look the way they imagined it.

How to access information

While 'information' is the 'I' of ICT, and vast amounts of it are accessible to us, it has become ever more important for us to show learners how to access and use it. Internet searching is less like using a library and more like a visit to a Wild West fair – all of life is there. Among the genuine teachers and the upstanding members of the community are the charlatans, the quack doctors, the frauds and the misguided amateur enthusiasts. But with guidance, learners can access a rich store of information. The challenge for us as teachers is twofold: first, to equip the children with skills to be able to seek information and to evaluate the worth of that which they find; and second, to recognise that we can no longer be the gate-keeper to all the information that our children may discover.

Relate the activity to the learner's experience

This aspect of andragogy is the least applicable to young learners as they will have had fewer experiences. If we borrow from the Foundation stage and the 'play-based' curriculum, we know that young learners' experience is rooted in play, and by relating activities to playful contexts we can help learning make sense (see *Learning ICT in English* project 5; *Arts* project 8; *Science* project 6). By using ICT in a context that relates to their experience we are able to develop children's abilities and understanding. We should also recognise that ICT is part of children's experience. The chart in each of the books in this series, relating the projects to the QCA scheme of work units, shows how we have aimed to embed the activities in meaningful contexts to enable children to access key ideas at earlier stages in their development.

Ready and motivated to learn

ICT can be helpful in overcoming inhibitions as the provisional nature of the medium allows corrections to be made to any work (see *Learning ICT in English* project 3, *Arts* project 4, *Maths* project 9). The motivational aspects of ICT are well documented (e.g. Passey *et al.* 2004), although we need to be cautious when relying on motivation as a sole justification for ICT. The technology is not, of itself, necessarily motivating. As computers become ubiquitous and accepted as a part of the way the world is, the challenges that we present to children in the tasks and projects that we plan need to intrigue and motivate them.

Help them overcome inhibitions

For many children this is not only an issue that relates to ICT, but we need to be sensitive to children as they learn the power of the medium. It was certainly the advent of word processors that enabled many of us to overcome our inhibitions and learn to type. Seeing that a text full of errors could be easily edited released us from the tyranny of the typewriter and encouraged us to persevere. Recognising that fundamental changes can be made to the appearance of text and images on the screen, and then undone, was hugely liberating, both in terms of the generation of ideas and in the evaluation of the work. The temporary nature of digital ink and paint also facilitates teacher–learner collaboration, as teachers can model possible developments to children's work by making changes on the screen and then removing them to let the child evaluate and decide how to proceed.

There is an understandable reluctance among teachers to adopt models designed for adults when considering ways to help children learn. The theorists described at the start of this chapter fought for the recognition of childhood as a discrete phase of development. Indeed, the recent emphasis on the development of early years education and the 'play-based curriculum' has been, in part, a reaction to the undue haste to prepare children for formal education and assessment in the UK. There are many aspects of the andragogic, learner-centred model that recommend it, even for very young learners, especially if we ensure that our activities are related to the learners' experience through play contexts. Indeed, our ability to develop new technologies and learn how to access the ever-growing amount of information rests upon the adoption of a more learner-centred model of education that will produce learners who are able to decide what should be learned, when and how, without relying on teachers to decide (Conner 1996). The central role of 'independent choice' throughout the projects described i̶ discussed in the next chapter.

ICT and multimodal learning

Much has been said about 'learning styles' as our understanding o̶ how the brain works has grown in recent decades. We have moved from theories of universal stages of learning (Piaget 2001) to learning styles (Honey and Mumford 1986) to visual, auditory or kinaesthetic types of learner and preferred individual modes of representation, as theories of neuro-linguistic programming (Dilts 1998; Craft 2001) have been applied to education. Many children will confidently inform you what type of learner they are, following assessment in school. A recent project at Trinity College Dublin (Kelly 2003) even used a learning style assessment to tailor the types of resources that would be displayed to each student on the university network when they logged on.

Armed with increasing knowledge of how children perceive the world and the concepts that we are trying to teach, the question is, What we do about it? Whereas it may be appropriate for a university to present information to students and adult learners in a way that matches closely the way that they are best able to understand it, should we do the same for children? Take those helpful diagrammatic representations of how to assemble Swedish furniture; they deliberately use no words so that they do not need to be translated into every language. For visual learners these may be fine, but for those who prefer instructions in text, this type of visual guide is less helpful. Similarly, some stages of the construction process need more precise explanation than can be given through a diagram that is open to misinterpretation.

The response to this issue in an educational context is to recognise a child's preferred representational mode and make sure that his or her ability to access the widest range of forms of information is developed; that is to adopt a multimodal strategy when presenting and developing ideas with children – not solely because any group of children is likely to contain individuals with a variety of styles and preferred modes of representation, but also because a learner's behaviour is contingent on many factors including the task and the social context. By exploiting the full range of modes of representation we can ensure that children are able to access learning in the way that makes most sense to them at that time and, at the same time, to be exposed to alternative modes.

With the advent of affordable, child-friendly, digital video, photography, music and a huge amount of on-line resources, ICT has become a hugely important tool for children to experience multimodal, multimedia learning (see *Learning ICT in the Arts* project 10; *Humanities* project 9; *Science* project 8; *English* project 4). The real power of the technology is the way in which very young children can become

...ors and creators of information in a range of modes, as well as readers, audience and critics.

Honey and Mumford (1986), when categorising types of learners as Activists, Reflectors, Theorists and Pragmatists, usefully described ways in which each type learned best. Table 1.1 identifies how integrated ICT activities can provide multimodal opportunities to address all the types of learners that they describe.

Table 1.1 Learning styles and ICT projects

Activists	
Activists learn best when:	**Projects in the subject books where there are opportunities for this**
there are new experiences or problems or opportunities	Arts 1 Maths 8, 9 Humanities 1, 4 Science 9 English 5, 6
there is excitement or drama or crisis, things chop and change and there is a range of diverse activities to tackle	Arts 10 English 3, 6, 8, 10 Maths 6, 8, 10 Humanities 4, 7
they have high visibility (e.g. can chair meetings, lead discussions, give presentations)	Arts 10 English 4, 7, 10 Maths 3, 4, 6, 9, 10 Humanities 7, 8, 9
they are 'thrown in at the deep end' with a task they think is difficult	Science 6, 9 English 3, 8, 10 Maths 7, 10 Humanities 5
they work with other people, e.g. in a team	Arts 10 Science 9 English 2, 3, 4, 6, 7, 8, 9, 10 Maths 4, 5, 6, 8, 10 Humanities 2, 3, 5, 7
it is appropriate to 'have a go'	Arts 1 Maths 3, 4, 7, 8, 9 Humanities 8 English 1, 2, 5, 9
Reflectors	
Reflectors learn best when:	**Projects in the subject books where there are opportunities for this**
they are allowed, or encouraged, to watch, think or 'chew over' activities	Arts 1 Maths 2, 3, 4, 7, 8, 9 Humanities 1, 5, 7 English 2, 3, 4, 5

Reflectors	
Reflectors learn best when:	**Projects in the subject books where there are opportunities for this**
they can stand back and listen or observe	Arts 1 Maths 1, 4, 6, 7, 8 Humanities 1, 3, 4, 8 English 1, 2, 3, 6, 7, 8
they are allowed to think before acting	Arts 1 Science 6 Maths 1, 3, 5, 7, 9, 10 Humanities 1, 2, 5, 8 English 3, 5, 9
they can carry out some painstaking research	Arts 7 Science 9 Maths 6, 10 Humanities 3, 5, 6, 8 English 5, 9, 10
they have the opportunity to review what has happened or what they have learned	Arts 1 Science 6 Maths 1, 4, 5, 7, 8, 9 Humanities 1, 5, 8, 9 English 2, 3, 4, 6, 7, 10
they are asked to produce carefully considered analyses and reports	Science 9 Maths 6, 8, 9, 10 Humanities 3, 5, 6, 8 English 5, 6, 9, 10
they are helped to exchange views in a structured situation	Science 6 Maths 6, 8, 9, 10 Humanities 5, 7 English 3, 6, 9, 10
they can reach a decision in their own time, without pressure and tight deadlines	Arts 7 Maths 5, 10 Humanities 6 English 9

Theorists	
Theorists learn best when:	**Projects in the subject books where there are opportunities for this**
what is offered is part of a system, model, concept or theory	Science 6 Maths 7, 8, 9 Humanities 5, 8 English 5, 9, 10
they can explore associations and interrelationships between ideas, events and situations, methodically	Arts 7 Science 9 Maths 1, 4, 5, 6, 7, 8, 9, 10 Humanities 3, 6 English 3, 5, 10

Table 1.1 (continued)

Theorists	
Theorists learn best when:	**Projects in the subject books where there are opportunities for this**
they are intellectually stretched	Arts 7 Maths 7, 9, 10 English 6, 10
they are in structured situations, with a clear purpose	Science 9 Maths 1, 4, 5, 6, 7, 8, 9, 10 Humanities 3, 6 English 3, 5, 10
they can listen or read about ideas and concepts that emphasise rationality or logic	Science 9 Maths 1, 4, 5, 6, 7, 8, 9, 10 Humanities 3, 6 English 3, 5, 10
they can analyse and then generalise	Arts 7 Science 9 Maths 1, 4, 5, 6, 7, 8, 9, 10 Humanities 3, 6 English 3, 5, 10
they are required to understand and participate in complex situations	Science 9 Maths 1, 4, 5, 6, 7, 8, 9, 10 Humanities 3, 6 English 3, 5, 10
Pragmatists	
Pragmatists learn best when:	**Projects in the subject books where there are opportunities for this**
there is an obvious link between the subject matter and a problem	Arts 1 Science 6 Maths 3, 6, 8, 10 Humanities 2, 4, 6, 7, 9 English 6, 7, 8, 9
they are shown practical techniques	Arts 1, 10 Science 9 Maths 1, 3, 6 Humanities 9 English 4, 7, 8
they have a chance to try these out with coaching or feedback from a credible expert (who can do the techniques themselves)	Arts 1 Science 9 Maths 1, 3, 6 Humanities 9 English 4, 7, 8

The curriculum and what children learn

With the development of the Primary National Strategy in the UK there has been an emphasis on how children are taught the subject matter of the National Curriculum. Although, in theory, the content of the curriculum has not altered, nor the intention that the required curriculum should not take up all the time that a child spends in school in a week, in reality some subjects have suffered as a result of reduced teaching time as the spotlight of national scrutiny has focused on the teaching of core subjects (Ofsted 2005).

The overloaded primary curriculum

Some historians are referring to this current epoch as 'The Information Age', mainly as a result of our increased ability to use ICT to access, process and distribute vast amounts of information. One of the corollaries of this has been a growth in both content and sources for all curriculum areas. New possibilities have opened up in geography, for example, with current information from around the world. We understand global issues much more easily and we can access satellite images and web cameras. In history, national records are available on-line and we can access and interrogate census data. Many museums have virtual collections which enable children to access images and information that would, until recently, have been very difficult to obtain.

> When the National Curriculum was first proposed it was mooted that a primary document would be produced as the subject categories were not intended as a way of organising the timetable, but rather as an auditing tool for planning!

If you continue to consider all the additional knowledge and activities that could enrich each subject of the curriculum it is easy to see how the sheer quantity of activity can lead to overload. There is a paradox that is a product of the way that we have used traditional subject areas to classify the curriculum content: while, undoubtedly, each curriculum subject is growing, children are increasingly likely to find themselves duplicating tasks as different subject areas teach new methods of researching, designing, data-handling, communicating and presenting.

Along with the growth in existing subjects there are also calls to add new subjects. The UK government's strategy to include a foreign language for all key stage 2 children by 2010, for example, is not expected to replace or remove any existing subject areas. One possible way to deal with increases in curriculum

content is the planned integration of different subject areas in the ways that we have described in this series, as by this means we are able to teach more, not less.

The integration of domains of knowledge

Educational theorists have argued for over a century against the organisation of the school curriculum into separate domains of knowledge. The argument that an important part of a child's development is to relate different domains and make connections between them to shape a cohesive view of the world has been put forward by those who see subjects as artificial constructs created and formed by political needs (Froebel, cited in Palmer 2001; Eisner 1992; Drake 1993). Early in the twentieth century, separate subject disciplines were viewed by some involved in the progressive education movement as obstructive to children's perception of the relationships between domains. The dislocation of the curriculum, they argued, led to a perceived lack of relevance, by the learners, of the discrete content areas. There is nothing natural about the current accepted organisation of curriculum content; children finding out about their environment do not consciously signal changes in their thinking as they ask 'geographical' questions about their locality, or 'scientific' questions about their environment, or use 'mathematical' or 'ICT' skills to measure and record.

Calls for the integration of curriculum subjects, then, are not new. The expectation for ICT learning to be taught across the curriculum, particularly in the primary phase, has been the position adopted by the UK National Curriculum since 1995. ICT tasks without a real purpose or context can be very sterile. The purpose of creating links between subjects is to bring meaning to the task and to help it make sense to children. Indeed, one of the approaches within the strategies for teaching literacy and numeracy in the UK has been to advocate links across subjects and so contextualise these key skills.

As the core subjects are high status, there has tended to be one-way traffic with this type of integration, with maths and English outcomes being incorporated in ICT lessons (and the other foundation subjects) rather than the other way round. Despite the fact that many ICT activities help children to make sense of the core concepts (see *Learning ICT with Science* project 3, *Maths* project 5, *English* project 7), it seems heretical to usurp core subject time with ICT outcomes when so much rests on the performance of children in the UK in the assessed and monitored aspects of the curriculum. As a result, rather than extending the time spent on foundation subjects, there is evidence that this type of one-way integration is reducing it, as we place undue emphasis on the maths or English outcomes (Ofsted 2005). In addition to reducing time for foundation subjects it is possible that excessive emphasis on the core subjects is going to be counter-productive to our intention to raise core subject standards also. A child who is struggling with mathematical concepts may not need more maths teaching but a range of contextualised activities that demonstrate a purpose for those concepts in a meaningful way, especially where there is a common process that can be mirrored by the ICT application.

The processes of data-handling, creativity, design, enquiry and ICT

When considering duplication within the curriculum it is important to distinguish between the type of useful repetition that is found in a planned spiral curriculum and the unnecessary duplication of tasks in an unplanned or fragmented curriculum. Part of the reason for the overcrowded curriculum discussed above is the competing claims that different subject areas have for similar processes that can be transformed by the use of ICT. Whereas understanding of these processes can be progressively developed by encountering increasing levels of challenge in a range of curriculum subjects, there is also the danger of repetition and duplication. Through integrated planning, children's ability to handle data, for example, can be introduced in a design and technology context (*Learning ICT in the Arts* project 7), developed in a historical context (*Humanities* project 6) and explained in a mathematical context (*Maths* projects 6 and 10). Planning across curriculum boundaries in this way will help children to see relationships and increase the relevance of the activities to their learning.

Most processes can be supported by ICT at one or more stages, either at the initial stage (prepare), the development stage (process) or the sharing stage (present) (see Table 1.2).

Teaching for creativity is another key aim of primary education that can be transformed with ICT. Creative processes also intersect subject boundaries and require an integrated planning approach. Making connections between the similar approaches described in art, design & technology, music and other fields, and the process of creating novel solutions will help to reduce duplication, and using ICT helps to make that connection. The process of decision-making through modelling ideas using ICT and evaluating alternatives, when developed progressively in a variety of contexts, becomes clearer and more secure. Cropley (2001) suggests nine key attributes of teaching that foster creativity. Through using ICT in context we can contribute to that fostering of creativity as outlined below (Table 1.3).

Craft (2001), in her review of research into creativity for the QCA, identified key strategies that were found to be important in pedagogical approaches to promote creativity. Among them was the need to encourage the integration of subject areas. It is in the design of 'real' activities containing meaning that we can create a curriculum relevant to children.

Table 1.2 Processes that can be supported by ICT

	Data-handling	Design	Enquiry	Creative writing
Prepare	Data-logging Internet searching	Computer-aided drawing Internet searching Taking digital photographs	Internet searching Using maps Accessing sources	Internet searching Reading texts Using writing frames
Process	Using spreadsheets or databases to organise and sort	Modelling ideas using drawing software or spreadsheets	Organising information Modelling connections	Modelling ideas Using thesaurus Outlining and structuring
Present	Presenting graphical information and reports	Communicating design ideas and processes	Creating information sources using multimedia or digital video	Publishing on screen or paper

ICT and independent choices

It can be seen from the discussion thus far that empowering children to make choices is one of the driving forces behind the design of all the projects in this series. Exploiting the full potential of ICT to enable children to become powerful producers of original ideas, at all ages, in a safe and sustainable way is key to this approach. We are not advocating an unregulated, *laissez-faire* approach, far from it; but we do maintain that skills and understanding are developed through integrated activity, so that children are suitably supported to be able to make independent choices at all levels.

The argument to teach basic skills before children embark on original work does not apply solely to ICT development, and it is made at the macro and the micro levels. Some would see the entire primary phase as preparing children's basic skills to enable them to engage with the curriculum at the secondary phase. Our approach also aims to see children participate fully in their learning at all stages, but we believe that each stage should include a suitable degree of independent choice to help contextualise and explore the learning. Progression is not going to occur if we attempt to develop skills alone before any degree of independent choice is introduced. Independent choice is a necessary, empowering ingredient at all levels of education, and skilful teaching of skills and techniques ensures that children are well supported so that they are able to choose successfully (see Figure 2.1: A model of ICT capability).

Table 1.3 Creativity supported by ICT (adapted from Cropley 2001)

Teachers who foster creativity:	They use ICT to:	Projects in subject booklets where there are opportunities for this
encourage students to learn independently	find problems and solutions; explore data; model and try out ideas	Maths 6, 10 Arts 3, 7
have a co-operative, socially integrative style of teaching	share ideas around a screen or whiteboard; undertake collaborative projects	Science 7
do not neglect the mastery of factual knowledge	find out information and validate and test it using models	Humanities 6 Maths 8
tolerate sensible or bold errors	reveal thinking and justify reasoning behind errors	Arts 8 Maths 4, 7, 8 English 3, 5
promote self-evaluation	consider alternative decisions and evaluate the process and the effects	Arts 2, 3 Science 7 Maths 4, 7, 8 English 3, 5, 10
take questions seriously	enable children to investigate questions raised	Science 8, 9 Maths 6, 8, 10
offer opportunities to work with varied materials under different conditions	organise and present ICT in the widest range of formats, including still and moving images, text, tables and graphs	Arts all projects Science 3, 4, 7, 8 Maths 5, 8 English 4, 7, 8 Humanities 9
help students learn to cope with frustration and failure	put children in challenging situations where they can make and evaluate decisions	Arts all projects Science 6, 7, 8 Maths 4, 6, 7, 8, 10 Humanities 1, 5, 6, 8 English 3, 4, 6, 7, 8
reward courage as much as being right	model situations and support children making brave decisions when exercising independent choice	see 'Independent choice' in Chapter 2

Degrees of curricular integration

Like many aspects of education, separate subjects and an integrated approach are not mutually exclusive. When using ICT to achieve learning in other subject areas there are different degrees to which ICT can have an impact on teaching and learning (Bennett 1997; Ager 2000). At an initial level, the use of ICT supports the learning. The work may have little or no impact on the development of ICT capability and the lesson is very similar in structure and outcome to what it would be without ICT. For example, children could be measuring hand spans and recording the information in a table. Whether the table is on a computer or on paper makes little difference to the activity. At the second level, the use of ICT extends what would otherwise have been done. If the table described above is set up on a spreadsheet file with a graph already formatted (see *Learning ICT in Science* project 5) the children could see immediately the spread of the data and could begin to discuss it. The final level is described as transforming, or sometimes enhancing, the learning, where the structure of the lesson and the subject outcomes are rewritten, and the activity usually promotes the development of ICT capability. Data-handling activities can be transformed by the use of data-logging to collect data or access large datafiles across the internet. Equally, a multiple-user datafile (MUD) (see *Maths* project 6) enables live information from different groups of children working on separate computers to contribute simultaneously to a shared display on the interactive whiteboard.

In this series we are advocating not the teaching of subject knowledge through the use of ICT but the teaching of ICT in subject contexts. In a similar way the teaching and learning of ICT can be better served with some activities than with others. Activities that support ICT learning provide opportunities for children to practise skills and routines with which they are already familiar. Activities which extend ICT introduce new skills and routines or require children to select from their current knowledge of ICT to find the appropriate procedure in a new context with a degree of independent choice. The transformational activities involve children combining a range of ICTs and learning how to use them in order to answer questions and solve problems of their own, in ways that would not be possible without ICT. In order to plan this type of activity the relationship between the subjects and their respective outcomes is important.

The planning of symbiotic outcomes

We have discussed in this chapter the rationale behind the integrated approach to teaching ICT through the curriculum subjects. We have been at pains to point out that this is not some type of reactionary reversion to an undisciplined topic approach that claimed to develop many curriculum areas but, in truth, taught none well. Although we have argued that separate subject disciplines may be destructive to children's learning and, in particular, the development of creativity, the approach does not need the National Curriculum to be rewritten, but just to be used as it was intended, as an auditing tool for teachers rather than a blueprint for the timetable. Armed with a clear knowledge of what children need to be taught, we can move forward to carefully planned and integrated subjects.

There are clearly risks inherent in this strategy that children's understanding of distinctive concepts within separate subject areas may be compromised. If there is little connection between the subject learning and the use of ICT, then the activity will fail to have meaning for the children and the teacher might fail to achieve an appropriate balance in the lesson. Through careful planning of 'symbiotic' or mutually beneficial outcomes, the risk can be managed. It is not as hard as it might at first appear to ensure that the use of ICT is going to make a positive contribution to subject learning and that the subject context is going to make a positive contribution to ICT learning. For an example of some symbiotic parts of the National Curriculum programme of study for ICT, art & design and design & technology, see Table 1.4. While there will be different emphases at times throughout any project, careful planning can ensure that rich and meaningful learning takes place.

Summary

In this chapter we set out to explore beliefs about the way we think ICT can and should be taught, not presenting the 'answer' but sharing views that can be used to shape your own. We have outlined some of the thinking behind our approach to teaching ICT in the ways described in the projects. Principles of

Table 1.4 The relationship between the ICT, art & design and D&T programmes of study

National Curriculum programme of study for key stage 1		
ICT	Art and design	Design and technology
4 Reviewing, modifying and evaluating work as it progresses	3 Evaluating and developing work	3 Evaluating processes and products
Pupils should be taught to:	Pupils should be taught to:	Pupils should be taught to:
a. review what they have done to help them develop their ideas	a. review what they and others have done and say what they think and feel about it	a. talk about their ideas, saying what they like and dislike
c. talk about what they might change in future work	b. identify what they might change in their current work or develop in their future work	b. identify what they could have done differently or how they could improve their work in the future

how children learn, and our growing knowledge of learning styles, have been discussed and we have reflected on the content and structure of the curriculum in the UK.

We have also put forward ways in which careful integration can help us to balance coverage of the curriculum through finding symbiotic relationships between subjects. For while the subject structure can help to audit the breadth of the primary curriculum, if we do not make connections between subject areas, duplication can occur and valuable opportunities to contextualise learning and make sense of it to young learners will be lost.

References

Ager, R. (2000) *The Art of Information and Communications Technology for Teachers*. London: David Fulton Publishers.

Bennett, R. (1997) *Teaching IT*. Oxford: Nash Pollock.

Conner M. (with E. Wright, K. Curry, L. DeVries *et al.*) (1996) *Learning: The Critical Technology* (2nd edn). St. Louis, Miss.: Wave Technologies International Inc. (http://www.learnativity.com/download/Learning_Whitepaper96.pdf).

Craft, A. (2001) 'Neuro-linguistic programming and learning theory'. *The Curriculum Journal*, **12**(1), 125–36, Spring.

Cropley, A. J. (2001) *Creativity in Education and Learning*. London: Routledge.

DfES (2004) *Every Child Matters*. London: Department for Education and Skills.

Dilts, R. B. (1998) *Modeling with NLP*. Capitola, CA: Meta Publications.

Drake, S. M. (1993) *Planning Integrated Curriculum: The Call to Adventure*. Vancouver: Association for Supervision and Curriculum Development Planning.

Drake, S. M. (1998) *Creating Integrated Curriculum*. Thousand Oaks, CA: Corwin Press.

Eisner, E. (1992) 'The federal reform of schools: looking for the silver bullet'. *Phi Delta Kappan*, **73**(9), May, 722–3.

Honey, P. and Mumford, A. (1986) *The Manual of Learning Styles*. Maidenhead: Peter Honey and Alan Mumford.

Kelly, D. (2003) 'A framework for using multiple intelligences in an ITS', in *Proceedings of EDMedia '03*. World Conference on Educational Multimedia, Hypermedia and Telecommunications. Honolulu, HI.

Kelly, D. and Tangney, B. (2003) *A Framework for Using Multiple Intelligences in an ITS*. Proceedings of World Conference on Educational Multimedia, Hypermedia & Telecommunications (EDMEDIA), USA, pp.2423–30 (https://www.cs.tcd.ie/erite/publications/sources/EDMEDIA03Paper4.pdf)

Kennewell, S., Parkinson, J. and Tanner, H. (2000) *Developing the ICT Capable School.* London: RoutledgeFalmer.

Knowles, M. (1990) *The Adult Learner: A Neglected Species* (4th edn). Gulf Publishing Co.

Loveless, A. and Dore, B. (2002) *ICT in the Primary School.* Buckingham: Open University Press.

Ofsted (2005) *The National Literacy and Numeracy Strategies and the Primary Curriculum* (HMI 2395). London: Ofsted.

Palmer, J. (ed.) (2001) Fifty Major Thinkers on Education: From Confucius to Dewey (electronic resource). London and New York: Routledge.

Passey, D., Rogers, C., Machell, J. and McHugh, L. (2004) *The Motivational Effect of ICT on Pupils.* Department of Educational Research, Lancaster University. DfES Research Report RR523 (www.dfes.gov.uk/research/data/uploadfiles/ RR523new.pdf).

Piaset, J. (2001). *Psychologie de l'intelligence* (trans. M. Piercey and D. Berlyne). Electronic resource. London and New York: Routledge.

Selinger, M. (2001) 'Learning information and communications technology skills and the subject context of the learning'. *Journal of Information Technology for Teacher Education,* 10(1, 2).

Sharp, J., Potter, J., Allen, J. and Loveless, A. (2002) *Primary ICT: Knowledge, Understanding and Practice* (2nd edn). Exeter: Learning Matters.

Vygotsky, L. (1962) *Language and Thought.* Cambridge, MA: MIT Press.

Progression in ICT

Progression in any subject is about ensuring that children acquire skills, knowledge and understanding systematically, through activities that build on previous learning and provide achievable challenges. For ICT, which has practical as well as theoretical elements, this means making sure children get better at performing increasingly complex hands-on tasks and understanding ever more sophisticated ideas and concepts. Pupils' levels of skills, knowledge and understanding in relation to ICT has conventionally been termed their 'ICT capability', and progression in ICT can be defined by the increasing scope, sophistication and transferability of this capability. The National Curriculum identifies four aspects of ICT capability:

⊙ finding things out

⊙ developing ideas and making things happen

⊙ exchanging and sharing information

⊙ reviewing, modifying and evaluating work as it progresses.

Although not entirely mutually exclusive, these terms are useful in helping to clarify the subject content of ICT. The first three describe strands of learning and the fourth emphasises the importance of critical reflection on that learning. 'Finding things out' refers to ICT as a tool for acquiring, interpreting and preparing information. 'Exchanging and sharing information' relates to communication using a range of media. 'Developing ideas and making things happen' covers modelling, monitoring and control. The progression grids (see Tables 2.2–2.5) use these strands as a framework. The content of these grids, however, refers to our model of ICT capability, presented in Figure 2.1.

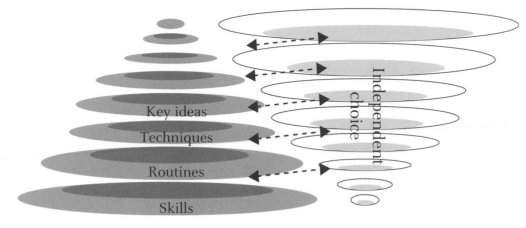

Figure 2.1 A model of ICT capability

A model of ICT capability

Our model of ICT capability operates at two levels. Globally, it shows how, through a series of ICT projects, from the Foundation stage to Year 6, pupils can attain a level of independent choice in relation to their use of ICT. On the left, the hierarchical cone formed by the skills, routines, techniques and key ideas of ICT, represents the content of the ICT projects described in the subject-centred books in this series. The cone's shape symbolises both the progression of activities within each project and the numerical relationships between elements of capability, e.g. the key ideas of ICT are relatively few in number compared to the number of basic skills that must be learned. In terms of the progression from Foundation stage to the top of key stage 2, the shape suggests that younger children will have a larger number of skills and routines to learn, before fully getting to grips with techniques and key ideas. Older children, who have mastered most basic skills

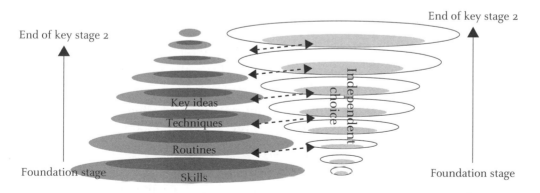

Figure 2.2 A model of ICT capability – the global level

and routines, will be able to focus more readily on techniques and a relatively small number of key ideas.

On the right, the inverted cone labelled 'independent choice' represents the growing range of choices available to pupils as they work through the projects. With each completed project, newly learned skills, routines, techniques and key ideas will add to a pupil's repertoire or capability in relation to ICT. The arrows linking the two cones illustrate the feedback between the projects and capability. Each completed project will add to children's independence and autonomy, leading to a confident response to challenges in subsequent projects. By the end of key stage 2, children will have a broadly based capability, enabling them to make informed choices about appropriate use of ICT in a wide range of contexts.

The global level of our model is best illustrated by the addition of labels (Figure 2.2).

At the *Foundation stage*, children will have a large number of basic ICT skills to learn and only limited independence and autonomy. By the *end of key stage 2*, experience in the projects will have led to a high degree of independence.

Components of capability

At a project-specific level our model shows the component parts of ICT capability building hierarchically upon each other and feeding directly into the development of children's autonomy in relation to ICT. At this stage it may be useful to define the meaning of terms in the model. Skills, routines, techniques and key ideas describe identifiable types of knowledge and understanding demanded by ICT as a subject. Our model shares some terms with the DfES/QCA primary scheme of work for ICT – learning objectives in the scheme are classified into techniques and key ideas – but adds underpinning levels of capability.

Skills

At the most basic level of ICT capability are the interactions between the learner and computer hardware/software. These are skills – the fundamental underpinnings of competence, best described as repetitive behaviours that are relatively easy to learn and, once learned, become almost instinctive – for example, clicking an 'OK' button on screen to activate an action or selecting an item from a drop-down menu. Most of these skills are learned early on in the development of ICT capability, but there are some skill-like behaviours that are acquired as the learner encounters new hardware and software, e.g. pressing the buttons on a programmable toy or manipulating the controls of a digital video camera. In the context of project 6 in the *Humanities* book in the series, for example, children in Year 4 who are gathering information from a census datafile will learn to activate the search function of a database by identifying the appropriate button on a toolbar.

Routines

Routines are combinations of the basic skills used to perform simple tasks. For example, the process a learner uses to print a file is a routine. It involves more than one skill but, like a skill, it can become almost instinctive. In fact, once learned, a learner may only become aware of a routine when it is interrupted or changed by the requirements of hardware or software.

The process of saving an unsaved document or file is very much a routine – select 'Save As' from the File menu; type in a filename; click the 'Save' button. When a learner first encounters an image-editing program, however, the routine may require some modification, as many of these programs add an additional step to the process, by requiring the user to select a file format or quality for the saved image. Again, using project 6 in the *Humanities* book as an example, children will learn the routine of setting up a search in the chosen database software – clicking on a 'Search' button in the toolbar; entering a search term; adding to the search using Boolean operators (AND, OR, NOT); clicking on 'OK' to activate the search. At first, this routine will be unfamiliar and may require some step-by-step support (from the teacher or from a set of instructions on paper), but as children progress through the task – of finding information about a specific person in the census datafile, then others with the same surname, then others at the same address – they will become more competent and confident, until they reach the point that they no longer need to 'think through' the steps of the search process. It will have become a routine.

Techniques

Skills and routines are combined at the next level of ICT capability. If skills and routines can be defined as the underpinning elements of ICT capability, exploiting the commonalities of hardware and software, techniques vary according to the task and the software. They involve the selection and application of choices by the learner. The process of 'dragging and dropping' on-screen items is very much a routine, used by a plethora of Early Years software applications. Within the context of word-processing software, however, it is a technique – alongside others such as Cut and Paste – that the learner may choose in order to move a chunk of text around the screen. Unfamiliar software will require the learning of new techniques, underpinned by previously learned skills and routines – the creation of shapes in a vector drawing program will require the learning of a new technique, informed by skills and routines acquired from paint programs. Techniques are unlikely to become instinctive for the learner because they vary from task to task and program to program. Techniques are the explicit, deliberate manifestations of ICT capability.

Techniques have an element of refinement that does not readily apply to skills and routines. Where children can only 'get better' at performing routines by doing them faster, progression in relation to techniques may involve a number of factors. In a LOGO control program, for example, children may first learn to move the screen turtle to draw a shape by typing in direct commands. Later, they will learn that they can do the same thing automatically by writing and activating a simple program or procedure – the shape can be drawn and redrawn repeatedly without typing the commands over and over again. Both are techniques used to perform a task, but the latter is 'better' because it is not only faster, it is also more sophisticated, efficient and elegant (see *Learning ICT in Maths* project 7 or *Arts* project 8).

Use of techniques can also be subject to personal preference. In a word processor there are usually a number of ways of changing a block of text to bold or italic. Some children will prefer to select a command from a menu, some will highlight the relevant text and click a button on the toolbar and some will highlight the text and type a combination of keys on the keyboard. In this case, no technique is really 'better' than the other; personal preference will determine which technique is used.

Key ideas

Key ideas form the next level of capability; they describe the application of appropriate techniques to tasks and applications; they are the knowledge base of ICT; they describe the subject-specific understanding that gives ICT an identity as a subject. At one level, they describe mundane concepts about items of data, e.g. they can be transitory and unreliable. At another level they describe and define the contribution of ICT to learning and teaching: the facility to model events and actions or to make mistakes in forgiving environments. Some key ideas are context-specific, e.g. instructions must be sequenced in precise ways to control some events. Others are overarching, e.g. that on-screen artefacts and documents can be finished products.

Like scientific concepts, such as the reasons why some objects float and some sink, key ideas are not understood and accommodated in one step but develop through experience. As children encounter new tasks, new contexts and new software, the meaning of a key idea will grow and broaden to take in new understandings. In the same way that the concept of a chair is developed every time a new type of chair is encountered, a key idea will become increasingly complex and sophisticated as it is encountered in different situations and contexts. The key idea of a computer as a modelling tool is a good example of this. In the Foundation stage and Year 1, children will encounter web-based games and activities that allow them to make choices that produce different outcomes (see the first projects in the *Humanities*, *Arts* and *English* books in this series). In Year 2 they will be introduced to graphical modelling (*Arts* project 3) and exploring alternatives using 'concept cartoons' (*Science* project 3). In key stage 2, children will explore tessellation and symmetry using drawing or painting software (*Mathematics* project 5). They will explore a 'virtual reality' model of a place of worship (*Humanities* project 4). They will use a spreadsheet model to explore 'What if . . . ?' questions (*Arts* project 7; *Mathematics* projects 8 and 9). Each project will add to and enrich children's experience of modelling and redefine their concept of a computer model.

Independent choice

Independent choice describes a state of competence and confidence in relation to ICT skills, routines, techniques and/or key ideas, which is both achievable and, in some respects, unachievable. As children work through projects they will gain knowledge and understanding that they can apply in other contexts. They will be empowered to make appropriate choices and decisions about when and when not to use ICT. For example, after repeated and progressive experience of different types of computer models throughout the primary school, by Year 6 many pupils will be able to select an appropriate model independently to help them to meet a particular learning challenge – make a spreadsheet to investigate energy-saving practices in a home or a DTP document to experiment with layout and design of text and pictures. Independent choice is not a state of ICT nirvana, however, where there is no more that can be learned; even the most experienced or professional user of ICT will attest to the fact that they will, probably, never know everything about the software that they use every day. Technological innovations inevitably impact upon education, and new developments (or the repackaging of familiar technologies in new forms) constantly present new challenges.

In a more limited way, independent choice also describes an understanding of the transferability of capability, which children will develop project by project. A child in the Foundation stage who has learned the routine of dragging and dropping objects on screen can exercise choice in a number of ways: he or she can use 'My World' to sort objects; use a simple, stamp-based paint program to create images; and access a wide range of on-line games and activities. Independent choice is, therefore, not just an end-point for capability, but also describes the growing repertoire of abilities that children can employ across the curriculum and in their leisure activities.

The projects

At a project-specific level, our model of ICT capability shows clearly the intrinsic progression in each project. Initial activities focus on teaching necessary new ICT skills and routines. Later, techniques and key ideas are introduced, explored and developed. Throughout, learning contributes to the growing range of choices available to pupils and their increasing independence and autonomy. At this level, our model of capability can usefully be presented as shown in Figure 2.3.

The analogy of linked pulleys is useful; it illustrates how the content of a project (the left-hand pulley) drives pupils' growing autonomy and independent choice (the right-hand pulley). At some points in the development of ICT capability, independent choice will become the drive pulley – children will be motivated to engage in a project by their need to learn new skills or techniques, so that they can use them in other subjects and contexts. It is important to note that school-based ICT does not operate in a vacuum – even young children are confident users of technology in out-of-school contexts – and independent choice extends beyond the school to home and leisure activities.

Projects gain meaning by being located in subject contexts. Subjects provide lively and meaningful contexts for learning and for practising skills and routines that otherwise can be quite mundane. The skill of 'dragging and dropping' could be learned by moving any abstract shapes around on the screen, but it is given

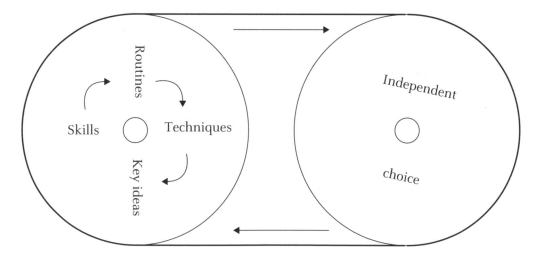

Figure 2.3 A model of ICT capability – the project level

meaning, relevance and purpose by sorting objects for Barnaby Bear (*Humanities* project 1), making pictures (*Arts* project 1), sorting images (*Science* project 1) or interaction with a talking book (*English* project 1). In the same way, key ideas gain resonance and significance by being located in a subject context. The task of communicating an impression of a place of worship brings key ideas about the interplay of video and sound to life and into sharp focus (*Humanities* project 9). Key ideas about presenting information for an audience are enlivened and enhanced through meaningful projects about authors (*English* project 9), contrasting localities (*Humanities* project 5) or a science topic (*Science* project 7). The teaching and learning of ICT are the *raison d'être* of our projects, however, and collectively they provide the progression that facilitates the development of ICT capability.

The progression grids

The charts on the following pages have a number of purposes:

- they gather together the learning objectives from the five subject books in the series

- they relate learning objectives to skills and routines, techniques and key ideas

- they map the learning objectives to the projects in the five subject books (for a complete list of the projects see the Appendix)

- they group the objectives with the National Curriculum ICT strands (finding things out; developing ideas and making things happen; exchanging and sharing information; reviewing, modifying and evaluating work as it progresses)

- they are structured around the levels in the National Curriculum attainment target for ICT and the early learning goal for ICT in *Curriculum Guidance for the Foundation Stage.*

These stages shown in the grids are not rigid and fixed, however; you may wish to consult grids 'below' or 'above' the age-range you are teaching to identify objectives, contexts or projects suitable for less experienced or more able pupils in your class. You may wish to consult the full range of grids to gain an overview of progression across the projects.

Although most learning objectives relating to skills and routines appear only once in the grids, learning objectives concerned with the development of

Table 2.1 Foundation stage and Year 1: early learning goals and level 1

	Finding things out	Sharing and exchanging information	Developing ideas and making things happen	General knowledge, skills and understanding
Skills and routines			Interact with text, images and animations through use of the mouse (English 1)	
			Drag items on screen (Art 1)	
			Control effects and actions on screen using mouse functions, e.g. clicking a mouse button, dragging and dropping (Humanities 1)	
			Small forward moves can be combined (i.e. the basis of addition) (Mathematics 1)	
			Backward moves negate forward moves (i.e. the basis of subtraction) (Mathematics 1)	
Techniques	Objects can be described, identified and sorted using keywords (Science 1)	Associate text with words and sounds (English 1)	Object-based drawing software can be used to model and present sorting activities (Science 1)	
	Use IT to test an hypothesis (Science 2)		Control devices must be programmed (Science 2)	
Key ideas	Pictures provide information (Science 1)	Ideas and thoughts can be communicated by using ICT tools (Art 1)	Devices that carry out repeated actions follow stored instructions which can include numbers (Science 2)	ICT is used in a variety of ways in the world around them (Art 1)
	Information can be collected from pictures and can be presented in a variety of forms (Science 2)	Computers can store and present information as text, pictures, sounds and moving images (English 1)	Programmable toys can be given instructions which they remember and can be changed (Mathematics 1)	ICT in learning is enjoyable and can be an interactive experience (Art 1)
		ICT can help to sort and present information (Science 1)	ICT makes it easy to correct mistakes and explore alternatives (Science 1)	
		ICT can be used to communicate ideas through pictures (Science 1)	Computers can represent real situations (Science 2) A computer representation allows the user to make choices and different decisions produce different outcomes (Humanities 1)	

Table 2.2 Years 1 and 2 (key stage 1): levels 1 to 3

	Finding things out	Sharing and exchanging information	Developing ideas and making things happen	General skills, knowledge and understanding
Skills and routines	Search using simple search terms (Humanities 3)	Interpret amounts of money displayed on screen (Mathematics 3)	Relate real objects to images on screen (Mathematics 3)	
	Select appropriate search results from a list (Humanities 3)	Select and use tools to make different marks on the page (Art 2)	Select, move, rotate and re-size graphic objects (Art 3)	
			Copy and paste parts of a 'painting' (Art 4)	
Techniques	Use hyperlinks to navigate around a visual information source (Humanities 4)	Communicate information about the size and differences between sets of objects (Mathematics 2)	Manipulate objects on screen in the context of a web-based activity or simulation (Humanities 3)	
	Gather information from a mainly visual information source (Humanities 4)	Enter text, images and sounds into a computer (English 2)	Manipulate objects on screen in the context of a web-based activity or simulation (Humanities 3)	
	Prepare data for a database, with an awareness that some questions have only yes/no answers and have to be phrased carefully (Science 1)	Use ICT appropriately to communicate ideas through text and images (Science 3)	Arrange and rearrange graphic objects on a page to create artwork (Art 2)	
		Pictures can be assembled by repeating elements (Art 4)	Images can be created by combining and manipulating objects (Art 2, 3)	
			Change colours and evaluate choices (Art 4)	
			Making marks on the screen using 'undo' makes it easy to correct mistakes and explore alternatives (Art 4)	
Key ideas	A tree diagram can be used to organise information and a branching database can be used to store and sort information which can be searched (Science 4)	ICT can be used to create pictures of different types, including map representations (Humanities 2)	ICT makes it easy to correct mistakes and explore alternatives (Humanities 2)	Effective maps use agreed or standardised symbols and ICT makes map-making easier (Humanities 2)

Table 2.2 (continued)

	Finding things out	Sharing and exchanging information	Developing ideas and making things happen	General skills, knowledge and understanding
Key ideas	A database can only answer questions if appropriate data have been entered (Science 4)	Objects can be represented by images, icons or blocks and despite the representation the same information can be deduced (Mathematics 2)	Explore options and make choices in the context of a computer representation of a real place (Humanities 4)	Supermarket tills are a form of computer (Mathematics 3)
	Objects can be divided according to criteria and collecting and storing information in an organised way helps them find answers to questions (Science 4)	Computers can be used to manipulate text, images and sounds (English 2)	Compare exploration of a computer representation of a place with first-hand experience (Humanities 4)	Computer-based talking stories are written by authors and not computers (English 2)
		ICT can be used to create pictures to present information (Science 3)	Objects can be classified and sorted into sets (Mathematics 2)	Evaluate a piece of work completed on a computer and suggest improvements (English 2)
		Artwork is provisional until printed (Art 2)	ICT makes it easy to correct mistakes and explore alternatives (Science 3)	Computers use icons to provide information and instructions (Science 3)
		A screen image can be a finished product (Art 4)	Images can be created by combining and manipulating objects (Art 4)	Information can be presented in a variety of forms and collected from a variety of sources (Art 2)
				Pictures can provide information and computers can represent real situations (Art 3)
				A computer representation allows you to make choices, explore alternatives and evaluate different outcomes (Art 3)

Table 2.3 Years 3 and 4 (key stage 2): levels 2 to 4

	Finding things out	Science sharing and exchanging information	Developing ideas and making things happen	Generic skills, knowledge and understanding
Skills and routines	Select a cell and add information to a spreadsheet (Arts 7)	Pictures can be assembled by repeating elements (Arts 5)	Design tessellating shapes using a paint program or a tessellation or tiling program (Mathematics 5)	Copy and paste information in text/ graphic form from one application (a web browser) to another (a DTP program) (Humanities 5)
	Interpret and analyse information in graphs (Science 6)	Use ICT appropriately to communicate ideas through text (Science 7)	Control a screen turtle (Mathematics 7)	
	Enter key facts into a database (English 5)	Record and check an audio recording (English 4)	Write and use LOGO procedures (Mathematics 7)	
	Search for records which meet particular criteria in a database (Mathematics 6)	Edit sounds with a simple sound-editing software package (English 4)	Create and use a spreadsheet model (Mathematics 8)	
	Present information as bar charts in a database (Mathematics 6)	Combine elements in a drawing program to create a finished image (English 5)		
	To create a simple database (Mathematics 6)	Write and respond to e-mails (English 6)		
	Select appropriate information from a web-based source (Humanities 5)	Add and open attachments to e-mails (English 6)		
		Transfer a chart/graph as an image from a database to a word-processed document (Mathematics 6)		
Techniques	Enter data in a spreadsheet and present findings (Science 5)	Images can be created by combining and manipulating photographs (Arts 5)	Explore the effect of changing the variables in a model and use them to make and test predictions (Arts 7)	Select suitable information and media and prepare it for processing using ICT (Science 7)
	Identify and correct implausible and inaccurate data (Science 5, 6)	Select and use different techniques to communicate ideas through pictures (Arts 5, Science 7)	Represent and plan a branching story as a flow chart (English 3)	Select skills and techniques to organise, reorganise and communicate ideas (Arts 6)
	Use ICT to classify information and present findings (Science 6)	Electronic and live sounds can be combined in a performance (Arts 6)	Reach collaborative decisions in the context of a branching story (English 3)	

Table 2.3 (continued)

		Finding things out	Science sharing and exchanging information	Developing ideas and making things happen	Generic skills, knowledge and understanding
		Use straightforward lines of enquiry (Science 6)	Use a multimedia authoring program to organise, refine and present information in different forms for a specific audience (Science 7)	The foundations of LOGO turtle graphics programming (Mathematics 4)	
		Work with others to interpret information (Science 6)	Create links between pages in a word processor (or multimedia/web authoring package) (English 3)	Apply knowledge of LOGO to solve given and self-created challenges and problems (Mathematics 7)	
		Interrogate a database with simple and combined searches (English 5)	Use the formatting features of a word processor to present a play script (including sound effects) (English 4)	Explore simulations systematically (Mathematics 8)	
			Evaluate a sound recording and suggest improvements (English 4)	Use a spreadsheet to investigate (Mathematics 8)	
			Use a drawing program (or tools) to explore symmetry and tessellation (Mathematics 5)		
Key ideas		Organising information can help to answer questions (Arts 7)	Images can be recorded, stored and transferred digitally (Arts 5)	Computer models enable alternatives to be explored and decisions to be evaluated (Arts 7)	Information comes from a variety of sources and can be presented in a variety of forms (Science 5, 7)
		Data represented graphically can be easier to understand than textual data (Science 5, 6)	Computer software can include a range of media which gives the user options to explore (Arts 5)	Simulations enable people to investigate 'What if . . .' situations (Mathematics 5, Arts 7)	ICT can be used for collecting, storing and sorting information in an organised way (Science 5, 6)
		Information can be represented as graphs but this can only provide limited answers to questions (Science 6)	ICT can be used to record and manipulate sounds to develop and refine a musical composition (Arts 6)	Regular shapes can be drawn using a repeated series of the same instructions (Mathematics 4)	Computers use icons to provide information and instructions (Science 7)
		Lines of best fit can suggest patterns and relationships between measurements (Science 6)	Sounds can be stored as computer files (Arts 6)	LOGO procedures comprise a series of instructions which can be amended (Mathematics 4)	To use ICT to organise, reorganise and analyse ideas and information (Science 7)
			A screen image can be a finished product (Science 7)		

	Finding things out	Science sharing and exchanging information	Developing ideas and making things happen	Generic skills, knowledge and understanding
Key ideas		ICT can be used to exchange information in text and image form (Humanities 7)		
		Web applications can be used to facilitate a dialogue between users in different locations (Humanities 7)		
		An awareness of audience is important when communicating using the internet (Humanities 7)		

Table 2.4 Years 5 and 6 (key stage 2): levels 3 to 5

	Finding things out	Sharing and exchanging information	Developing ideas and making things happen	Generic skills, knowledge and understanding
Skills and routines	Search a database, looking for specific information, using more advanced searching techniques (Humanities 6)	Insert images and sounds into a multimedia authoring program (Humanities 8)	Enter formulae into spreadsheets (Maths 9)	
	Interpret scattergraphs (Maths 10)	Use a digital camera (English 7)	Create and control multiple turtle shapes (Arts 8)	
	Interpret and analyse information in graphs (Science 9)	Basic digital photo editing (English 7)	Write repeating procedures to produce a desired outcome (Arts 8)	
	Use the tools in on-line search engines to find out the answers to specific questions (Science 10)	Create a linear presentation (English 7)		
		Use a digital video camera (English 8)		
		Use a digital video-editing software package (English 8)		
		Hyperlink web pages (English 9)		
		Record and edit video and view a frame at a time (Science 8)		

Table 2.4 (continued)

		Finding things out	Sharing and exchanging information	Developing ideas and making things happen	Generic skills, knowledge and understanding
Techniques		Use the tools of a database package to answer questions (Humanities 6)	Use a multimedia authoring program to refine and present information in different forms for a specific audience (Humanities 8)	Use spreadsheets to investigate functions and number patterns (Maths 9)	Structure information as part of a collaborative project (English 10)
		Search for images and sounds on the web using simple and more complex search strategies (Humanities 8)	Assemble a short digital video using still images, audio and text (Humanities 9)	LOGO procedures can call other procedures (Arts 8)	Select suitable information and media and prepare it for processing using ICT (Arts 10)
		Use a database (or spreadsheet) to analyse data (Maths 10)	Present information for a worldwide audience (English 9)	Write repeating procedures to produce a desired outcome (Arts 9)	
		Form and test hypotheses (Science 8, 9) (Maths 10)	Design and create a web page (English 9)		
		Conduct a statistical investigation using a database or spreadsheet (Maths 10)	Organise, refine and present information in different forms for a specific audience (Arts 10)		
		Locate, identify and access information on the internet to address specific lines of enquiry (English 10)			
		Line graphs can be used to show continuously changing information (Science 9)			
		Identify opportunities and design simple investigations for which the collection of data through a computer device is both feasible and advantageous (Science 9)			
		Use complex searches to locate information (Science 10)			

	Finding things out	Sharing and exchanging information	Developing ideas and making things happen	Generic skills, knowledge and understanding
Key ideas	To use a database (or spreadsheet) to analyse data (Maths 10)	Compare the presentation of information with multimedia to presentation by paper-based means (Humanities 8)	Spreadsheets can be used to explore the interrelationships between number operations (Maths 9)	Information can be presented using ICT (English 10)
	Video can be used to identify patterns and relationships (Science 8)	Digital video can be used to convey an impression of a place of worship, focusing on its character and symbolism (Humanities 9)	ICT makes it easy to explore alternatives (Arts 8)	Information comes from a variety of sources and can be presented in a variety of forms (Science 8, 9, 10)
	Video can be used to monitor changes in environmental conditions (Science 8)	Evaluate the effectiveness of a web page and a website (English 9)	Machines and devices are controlled and control devices must be programmed (Arts 9)	ICT can be used to store and sort information (Science 9)
	A video can be used to can-take samples of data for a set period of time (Science 8)	Data represented graphically can be easier to understand than textual data (Science 9)	Sequence affects outcome (Arts 9)	
	Information can be represented as graphs but these can only provide limited answers to questions (Science 9)	Information can be connected in different ways at the same time (Science 10)	Instructions can be recorded for replication and amendment (Arts 9)	
	Sensing devices can be used to monitor changes in environmental conditions (Science 9)	ICT can be used to develop images (Arts 8)	Recording a sequence of instructions forms the basis of control work (Arts 9)	
	A computer can take samples of data for a set period of time (Science 9)	ICT can be used to develop images and a screen image can be a finished product (Arts 10)	ICT makes it easy to arrange and reorder video clips and explore alternatives (Arts 10)	
	Searches can be carried out using more than one criterion (Science 10)	Pictures and sounds can be combined in a performance (Arts 10)		
	Understand the importance of choosing key words to find information (Science 10)			

Table 2.5 Overview of projects and National Curriculum levels

	Arts	Science	English	Mathematics	Humanities
Foundation stage; National Curriculum level 1	Arts 1: Building pictures	Science 1: Drag and drop sorting Science 2: Digital microscope – time-lapse	English 1: Using talking books	Mathematics 1: Using programmable toys Mathematics 2: Counting	Humanities 1: Decision making with a mouse
National Curriculum levels 1–3	Arts 2: Aboriginal art Arts 3: Designing an environment Arts 4: Designing logos Arts 5: Digital photos	Science 3: Concept cartoons Science 4: Branching database	English 2: Making talking books English 3: Branching stories and adventure stories English 4: Working with audio	Mathematics 3: Shopping Mathematics 4: Exploring with directions	Humanities 2: Map making using GIS software Humanities 3: Using an information source Humanities 4: A virtual tour of a place of worship
National Curriculum levels 2–4	Arts 6: Sound pictures Arts 7: Using a spreadsheet model	Science 5: Graphical representation of data Science 6: Giant's hand Science 7: Multimedia information source Science 8: Digital video – freeze-frame	English 5: Villains English 6: Imaginative e-mail English 7: Photo-dramas English 8: Digital video	Mathematics 5: Symmetry and tessellation Mathematics 6: Statistical investigations 1 Mathematics 7: LOGO challenges Mathematics 8: Modelling investigations	Humanities 5: Re-purposing information for different audiences Humanities 6: Using a database to analyse census data Humanities 7: Link with a contrasting locality Humanities 8: Making an information source
National Curriculum levels 3–5	Arts 8: LOGO animation Arts 9: Controlling external devices Arts 10: Creating a digital 'silent film'	Science 9: Data-logging Science 10: Using search engines	English 9: Creating an information website English 10: A *Macbeth* webquest	Mathematics 9: Patterns and spreadsheets Mathematics 10: Statistical investigations 2	Humanities 9: A video of a visit to a place of worship

techniques and key ideas may appear several times, with some modification on each occurrence. This is because many techniques and key ideas are unlikely to be developed fully through work in one project at one level. The repetition of the objective does not indicate repetition in terms of content, but reinforcement and development of an approach or concept. For example, the key idea 'ICT makes it easy to correct mistakes and explore alternatives' appears in the Foundation stage, level 1 grid in the context of sorting images in the first *Science* project. It reappears in the level 1–3 grid, again in a science context, when children are making concept cartoons. In the level 2–4 grid the context is spreadsheet modelling in *Arts* project 7 and, in the level 3–5 grid, it is *Arts* project 8 about LOGO animation. In working through these projects children will gain a broad and rounded understanding of the key idea, having experienced it in different contexts, at different times and using different software.

Summary

In this chapter we have focused on the nature of progression in ICT and our analysis of ICT capability. We have identified elements of capability in the form of skills, routines, techniques and key ideas. We have also described and explored the notion of independent choice as a target for children's learning in ICT in the primary school and as a developing manifestation of capability.

The grids outlining progression in ICT, through the projects in the subject books, from the Foundation stage to Year 6, have been explained and presented. These grids are central to this book and to the series in that they provide the underpinning for the discussion of planning, managing and assessing ICT, which follows in the next three chapters.

CHAPTER 3

Planning ICT

This chapter focuses on effective ways of planning ICT projects, lessons and activities. The suggestions are based on the core principle of this series: ICT capability is best developed through meaningful, subject-related contexts.

After defining some general planning principles for the systematic development of ICT capability, the chapter explores ways in which ICT can support classroom teaching, and ICT activities can be integrated into subject learning. Ideas for using ICT to support specific aspects of children's learning, and suggestions for planning an ICT project are given. Finally, there are sources of information, guidance resources and ideas.

General principles

The most effective way to develop pupils' ICT capabilities is to provide them with meaningful activities, embedded in purposeful subject-related contexts. For example, rather than teaching children how to use a database, a knowledge of database principles and processes and the skills required to enter and manipulate data, can be taught through using a database to help the children learn something useful about a subject. In *Learning ICT in English* project 5, for example, they find out how a database works by storing information about hypothetical villains. They then use the database to solve crimes. In *Humanities* project 6 the children use increasingly complex searches to interrogate census data so that they can find out what life was like in Victorian times.

Another core principle of our work is that the level of demand of most ICT activities can be adjusted to meet the needs of the children. For example, the learning outcome for a science activity could be for children to label a picture of a plant. Children with little experience of ICT could drag and drop labels from one part of the screen to another. Children with more experience could extract labels from a word bank, while yet more confident children might be expected to type the names in. The most advanced group could be expected to locate a suitable image from the internet or use a paint program to draw their own image. In terms of subject learning, the outcome for all these activities is broadly similar – a plant drawing is labelled – but in terms of ICT learning, the activity could be taught in several different ways to achieve quite diverse learning outcomes.

As we have seen in Chapter 2, ICT capability involves a good deal more than developing technical competence in the use of ICT equipment. ICT capability comprises:

- ⊙ skills – the basic building block of ICT capability; for example, using a mouse to control the pointer on a screen, or a keyboard to enter text

- ⊙ routines – a combination of basic skills; for example, the process of saving a file requires the combination of a series of skills. As with skills, routines will ultimately become automatic, unconscious events

- ⊙ techniques – involve the conscious choice of routines and skills to complete a task; for example, deciding whether a chunk of text will be copied and pasted, dragged and dropped or deleted and rewritten. Preferred techniques for achieving the same outcome may vary from person to person

- ⊙ key ideas – parcels of knowledge, concepts or ideas that are specific to ICT; for example, the difference between a flat-file database and a branching database is a key idea that can be learned by rote or through experience. A feature of key ideas is that some can be learned from experience and others have to be taught

- ⊙ independent choice – the ultimate aim of any teacher is to provide pupils with a repertoire of knowledge and skills and the understanding required for these to be applied to solve problems with minimal assistance. By the time the children leave primary school it is to be hoped they will be able to make informed decisions about the most appropriate application of ICT for a given task

- ⊙ projects – require the combination of skills, routines, techniques and key ideas to achieve a discernible outcome; for example, creating a simple branching story (*Learning ICT in English* project 3) is a project that entails the application of several routines and techniques and requires the appreciation of several key ideas.

Although there is a hierarchical structure to these aspects of capability, it should not be assumed that children cannot engage in projects until they have developed competence in all the necessary skills, routines or techniques. Although some preliminary teaching might be required, carefully structured teaching should enable the children to develop basic skills and key ideas through engagement with a project. ICT capability is best developed on a 'need to know' basis.

In summary, the core principles of our approach to planning ICT-based activities are that:

- ICT capability is best developed in the context of purposeful subject-related contexts

- the level of ICT challenge can be adjusted in most activities to suit the needs of the learner without affecting the subject outcomes

- although there is a hierarchical structure to ICT capability, projects can be organised to provide opportunities for basic skills and knowledge to be acquired on a 'need to know' basis.

Planning for progression

One of the greatest problems facing the primary teacher is planning ICT activities that can help the children develop their ICT capabilities. Sometimes the difficulties are associated with a teacher's lack of confidence with ICT and hence uncertainty as to what should be expected of children using ICT resources. Alternatively, the teacher can be quite confident with ICT but uncertain as to how the ICT activities can be structured for progression across a series of different applications. For example, if the focus for one term is on databases and for the next term is on word processing, how can progression be planned into the programme of activities? Similarly, if ICT is to be integrated across the learning in several subjects, how can progression of ICT capability be assured?

The subject projects are at the heart of these books. Each project demonstrates how ICT capability can be developed within the context of various subjects. You will have noticed that there is an overlap between projects in different books; for example, digital video can be found in *Science* project 8, *Humanities* project 9, *English* project 8 and *Arts* project 10. As a teacher you have a choice as to which subject context you could use to develop the children's capabilities in the use of digital video, if this is an objective for your teaching.

A key feature of our rationale for the projects is the notion that the level of ICT demand can be adjusted to suit the needs of the learner. We have suggested target age-groups for our projects, but we have also indicated how they can be modified to cater for the needs of more or less experienced children. Your choice of project does not need to be restricted to that shown for your particular age-group. It is probably an exaggeration to say that every project could be adapted to be used with any age-group; most can be used with the majority of primary children, provided the level of support or challenge is suitably modified.

A four-stage approach to planning ICT

When planning for the integration of the projects into your teaching, we suggest using the following approach:

1. Determine the ICT teaching objectives for the planning period (year/term/half-term).

2. Clarify key topics for each subject for the planning period.

3. Identify opportunities for ICT within each subject.

4. Select and adapt the ICT projects which are most appropriate for achieving the ICT objectives with the subject contexts. The tables in Chapter 2 give an overview of the key skills and ideas covered by the projects.

Case studies

The following three case studies are provided to exemplify how the projects could be used to develop ICT capability in different teaching situations:

⊙ a Year 3 class in a school with well-defined long-term planning for ICT

⊙ a Year 3 class in a school which uses the QCA scheme of work for ICT

⊙ a Year 5 class in a school with a loosely defined scheme for ICT.

A Year 3 class in a school with well-defined long-term planning for ICT

The ICT teaching objectives for the term
⊙ word-processing skills – entering text, changing font and size, copying and pasting

⊙ image-handling – creating simple pictures for insertion into word-processed documents.

Key topics for each subject for the term

⊙ literacy – storywriting; characters in poetry; class dictionaries; flow charts

⊙ numeracy – counting; properties of number; place value; order; money; measures

⊙ science – plants and growth

⊙ geography/history – locality study; what has changed; where we live

⊙ art – drawing and painting from life; Van Gogh

⊙ D&T – levers and linkages; pop-up mechanisms

⊙ music – singing; rhythm.

Opportunities for ICT within each subject

The teacher decided that the most promising opportunities for incorporating ICT were:

⊙ literacy – word processing stories or parts of stories; drawing characters for illustrating the stories

⊙ science – digital photos to record plant growth; pasting photos into word-processed accounts

⊙ geography/history – digital photos of locality; written/illustrated accounts of significant human and environmental features of the locality

⊙ art – manipulation of digital photos to replicate some of Van Gogh's effects.

Projects most appropriate for achieving the ICT objectives

The teacher decided to draw upon the ideas in the following projects and adapt them to meet her teaching objectives for the term:

⊙ *English* project 2 – Talking books. The ICT sessions for the first half-term would be used to work on a class-talking story. The children would work in pairs to produce their own illustrated page.

⊙ *Humanities* project 2 – Map-making using GIS. The children would draw a map of their locality and illustrate key features with digital photos taken on a field trip. They would incorporate their own reports of the features. This would lead to a wall display.

In addition, during the second half-term the children would use a digital camera to record the growth of their bean seeds. A template document would be used to encourage the children to be systematic in their recording of the seeds' growth. The classroom computer would be used at least twice during each week by each group in turn to complete their record.

The teacher decided that the focus for the first half-term would be on word-processing skills and the use of a paint program to produce the illustrations for the class story. The second half-term would concentrate on taking, editing and using digital photos for the art and science activities.

A Year 3 class in a school which uses the QCA scheme of work for ICT

The ICT teaching objectives for the year

⊙ Autumn term – Unit 3A: Combining text and graphics; Unit 3D: Exploring simulations

⊙ Spring term – Unit 3C: Introduction to databases; Unit 3E: e-mail

⊙ Summer term – Unit 3B: Manipulating sound.

Key topics for each subject for the year

Autumn term

⊙ literacy – story settings; dialogue; play scripts; non-chronological writing

⊙ numeracy – place value; estimating; money; measures

⊙ science – Unit 3C: Characteristics of materials; Unit 3D: Rocks and soils

⊙ history – Unit 10: What can we find out about ancient Egypt from what has survived?

⊙ art – Unit 3B: Investigating pattern

⊙ D&T – Unit 3A: Packaging

⊙ music – Unit 9: Animal magic; exploring descriptive sounds.

Spring term

⊙ literacy – story planning; character profiles; traditional stories; instructions; note-taking

- numeracy – rounding; money; fractions; handling data
- science – Unit 3A: Teeth and eating; Unit 3B: Helping plants grow well
- geography – Unit 18: Connecting ourselves to the world
- citizenship – Unit 05: Living in a diverse world
- art – Unit 3A: Portraying relationships
- D&T – Unit 3B: Sandwich snacks
- music – Unit 10: Play it again; exploring rhythmic patterns.

Summer term

- literacy – story planning; expanding skeleton stories; book reviews; poetry; recounts; letter writing
- numeracy – multiplication/division; problem-solving; time; handling data
- science – Unit 3E: Magnets and springs; Unit 3F: Light and shadows
- geography – Unit 6: Investigating our local area
- history – Unit 6A: A Roman case study
- art – Unit 3C: Can we change places?
- D&T – Unit 3C: Moving monsters
- music – Unit 11: The class orchestra; exploring arrangements.

Opportunities for ICT within each subject

Autumn term

- literacy – word processing; adding images to text
- science – branching databases; sorting and classifying
- history – internet searching; repurposing information from the Web
- art – tiling and pattern-making
- D&T – exploring different designs using a drawing or painting package
- music – audio recording; sound effects.

Spring term

- literacy – word processing; editing text; expanding notes

- numeracy – databases; money activities

- science – analysing nutritional data; logging growth with spreadsheet; digital photos of plant growth

- geography – internet searching; e-mail

- citizenship – internet searching; e-mail

- art – manipulating digital photos

- D&T – using modelling software to design the perfect meal

- music – music software to explore patterns in sound.

Summer term
- literacy – editing to improve skeleton stories

- numeracy – problem-solving software; databases

- science – data-logging; light and sound

- geography – digital photography; combining digital images and text; presentation software

- history – digital photos from Roman visit; internet sources of information; repurposing information

- art – digital photography; designing artefacts

- D&T – internet research on monsters; simulation (design a monster)

- music – music software; composing/arranging musical phrases.

ICT projects most appropriate for achieving the ICT objectives

The brainstorming of opportunities for ICT produced several possibilities which the teacher could have decided to pursue. However, as the school policy was to follow the QCA schemes of work she selected those projects and/or units which would enable the children to achieve the same or similar learning outcomes by the end of the year.

Autumn term
- *Science* project 3 – Concept cartoons. Linked with the science work on materials and rocks, the children combine text and graphics to portray their understanding of materials and their origins.

- *Maths* project 8 – Modelling investigations. The teacher selects on-line simulation activities which tie in with the numeracy work on measures and the science work on materials.

- *Arts* project 4 – Designing logos. A one-lesson activity related to the children's D&T work on packaging.

Spring term

- *Maths* project 6 – Statistical investigations 1. To support the work in numeracy lessons on data-handling and also work in PE and PHSE on healthy living.

- *English* project 6 – Imaginative e-mail. This project supports the work planned for geography and citizenship and acts as a preliminary to the planned activities for the Summer term on contrasting localities. The school used for the e-mailing project will be used for comparing information about localities.

Summer term

- *Arts* project 6 – Sound pictures. Ties in with planned work for music and for science. Creating, sampling and manipulating sounds.

- *Humanities* project 7 – Link with a contrasting locality. Relates closely to the planned work for geography and builds on the work started in the previous term on e-mail by introducing the children to blogging.

A Year 5 class in a school with a loosely defined scheme for ICT

The ICT teaching objectives for the half-term

The school's long-term planning for ICT is quite flexible. Teachers can draw upon any ICT activity which they feel is appropriate for the subject work they are teaching. However, the school has a very well developed record-keeping system to ensure that the children make continuous progress with the development of their ICT skills. The teacher's records show that the children have already achieved the following:

- Finding things out. All the children are accomplished users of the internet and can search for and download text and graphics. They all know the differences between branching and flat-file databases and, with a little guidance, can create their own databases. They have some knowledge of spreadsheets, but most have only used them for entering data and making graphs. The most able have used formulae but in limited ways (e.g. SUM).

⊙ Developing ideas and making things happen. Their previous teacher was very keen on control and so the children have built their own fairground models which they have controlled via a flow-charting program. Some children have used feedback in their control programs. All children have created multimedia presentations of branching stories and a simple class-based information source. They have not incorporated sound or animation into multimedia presentations.

⊙ Sharing and exchanging information. The children are all accomplished users of word processors and a desktop publishing program. They have edited digital photos using a range of effects and have edited videos. Some have manipulated sound to create sound effects for their video productions. They have not yet created web pages or used e-mail.

Key topics for each subject for the half-term

The school follows the literacy and numeracy frameworks in outline, but teachers are encouraged to address the identified needs of the children. Detailed and accurate record-keeping underpins the work they do, tracking each child's progress through the subjects. Cross-curricular topics are planned for each half-term (sometimes a full term). The theme for this half-term is Light.

⊙ literacy – play scripts; poetry about light and dark

⊙ numeracy – place value; mental methods (× and ÷); fractions (linked with phases of moon, calendar, etc.); data-handling

⊙ science – light; colour; sight; changes of state (burning); electricity

⊙ history – World War 2

⊙ art – Impressionism; digital photography; Rangoli patterns

⊙ D&T – torches; lamps; lights; burglar alarms; photocells

⊙ RE – Diwali and festivals of light

⊙ PE – dance sequences

⊙ music – 'light' music.

Opportunities for ICT within each subject

⊙ literacy – researching myths and legends; word processing and DTP

⊙ numeracy – researching calendars; Moon's phases; planet distances (large numbers); relationships between orbits; day length; distance from Sun

- science – data-logging (light); research as for numeracy

- history – information-gathering; video/photo-dramas

- art – manipulating digital images (Impressionism)

- D&T – control using sensors (light/infra-red)

- RE – research and presentation

- PE – plotting dance sequences; video

- music – digital composition for dance sequences.

ICT projects most appropriate for achieving the ICT objectives

- *Humanities* project 8 – Making an information source. The children will contribute to a multimedia presentation about World War 2 using images, sounds and re-enactments of home life during the war. Some elements will be presented on the school's website.

- *Science* project 7 – Multimedia information source. They will create a multimedia information source about a voyage around the solar system, including numerical data about planets' orbits.

- *English* project 7 – Photo-dramas. Some groups will contribute photo-dramas to the WW2 presentation about home life during the war.

- *Arts* project 5 – Digital photos (one lesson). The children will manipulate photos taken around the school grounds (last term) to create Impressionist pictures.

Although this may seem like an ambitious undertaking for one term's work, you will notice that three projects are mutually supportive. Some children will be focusing on the World War 2 presentation while others will be involved with the science project. Both groups will be developing the same skills in multimedia authoring. The photo-dramas will relate to their literacy work and will contribute to their work in history.

Challenging children

A concern which has been expressed repeatedly by Ofsted is that while there has been an improvement in recent years in the quality of ICT teaching and learning, all too often ICT activities are taught in isolation from other subjects:

Although many schools have made great strides in the teaching of ICT capability, the use of ICT frequently does not have sufficient impact on *teaching and learning in other subjects.* (Ofsted 2004a: 5–6, document's emphasis)

By adopting the 'four-step' approach used above, it should be possible to integrate ICT across the curriculum and continue to systematically develop children's ICT capabilities through adjusting the level of support and challenge.

Another feature of ICT work which has been identified in successive Ofsted inspections has been a lack of challenge. Some teachers are inclined to be too accepting of the children's work, missing opportunities to increase the level of challenge which the children could be capable of achieving:

Although there have been significant gains in the quality of teaching using ICT, a continuing issue is the lack of challenge presented to pupils in many lessons. Often this is because teachers have not gauged the ICT capability of pupils; for instance 'home users' are often more capable than the teacher realises. Furthermore, pupils sometimes learn a skill more quickly than anticipated, and then spend time practising something unnecessarily. (Ofsted 2004b: 8)

There are plenty of examples of key stage 1 children creating multimedia presentations and digital videos – see the Becta Digital Media Creativity Awards website for examples (www.becta.org.uk). If young children are capable of creating and presenting information using these media, what should be expected of the same children by Year 6?

Gauging the level of challenge for ICT activities can be difficult, particularly as the children progress through key stage 2. Some children may be highly proficient when using one piece of software but inexperienced with another. However, you will generally find that a child who is a confident user of ICT will be able to transfer knowledge and skills across software packages. Often the greatest barrier which children (and most teachers) have to overcome is recognising that it is quite hard to damage a computer – it will simply tell you that you have made a mistake and allow you to put it right. The difference between confident users of ICT and inexperienced ones is that confident users have a greater repertoire of knowledge from which to draw. They will continue to try things out until eventually something happens; either the computer carries out the required task or it does not.

Increasing the level of challenge does not necessarily mean doing something which is technically more advanced. The level of challenge could relate to the subject content, or the style and mode of presentation. For example, if a pair of children is working on a slide for a presentation, you could ask them whether they have thought about changing the size of the text, including another picture or modifying the content of the text so that it makes more sense.

However, to enable children to make good progress with the development of their ICT capabilities it will be necessary to intervene on occasion to suggest a more advanced technique or to show them a feature of the software which could enable them to be more productive in their use of time.

All the projects shown in the subject books in this series include suggestions for ways of raising the level of challenge for older or more capable children. The 'What do I need to know?' sections provide guidance on some of the technical aspects which you and the children need to master in order to complete the tasks. However, because we are unable to predict precisely which piece of software you will be using, you may have to experiment with a program or application to find out how it works. If you lack confidence with ICT, our advice is to focus on a small number of programs, preferably those which are flexible in their application, such as a word processor, an image-editing package and a database. Try to master these programs, so that when the children come to use them you have rehearsed their tasks to an extent whereby you are able to cope with most problems and issues that might arise. You can never be prepared for the unexpected, but gaining confidence with the software will help.

Most educational software provides the user with plenty of support and guidance. If you are struggling, draw support from whichever of the following might be the most helpful:

⦿ the manual for the software – it has usually been written with the 'average' teacher in mind

⦿ the on-screen help menu – most programs include on-screen help, either designed for the pupil or the teacher

⦿ experimentation – computers are quite happy to provide you with feedback if you make a mistake; keep trying things until something happens; if in doubt, close the program; as a last resort, turn off the computer (hold in the power button for five seconds on most computers)

⦿ the children – if you get stuck, ask if any children have found a way of solving the problem; if they have not, they might be able to suggest a strategy which they have developed for tackling similar problems

⦿ a colleague – others on the staff may have experienced the same problem and found a solution; the ICT co-ordinator might know what to do, or might know a colleague in another school who could help

⦿ a friend – one of your friends might be quite a confident user of computers and might be able to find a solution or interpret the manual if you are finding it particularly unhelpful

⊙ the internet – visit the software company's website to see if there are any help files. If it is a problem to which you can find no solution, send them an e-mail asking for advice. They are usually very responsive; most educational software suppliers rely on recommendation by teachers to other teachers to spread the word about their products.

Using the projects

The projects in the subject books are self-contained; all the information you need is contained within them and any additional resources you may require are provided on the accompanying CD-ROM. If you have used the four-step approach to identify the most appropriate projects for your subject teaching, you should next:

⊙ read through the project outline to see what resources, skills and knowledge you will need

⊙ plan any preparatory activities that might be needed for the related subject(s) to, for example, ensure that the content needed will be available when the children need to work in the computer suite

⊙ practise or test-run the activities in the project(s), paying particular attention to any task with which you are unfamiliar

⊙ prepare any resources, files or support materials needed for the activity – for example, some database activities may need a blank datafile setting up before the lesson (many of the resources needed are on the CD-ROM).

Resources

Some projects use a particular program, but these are generally examples of a type of program. The guidance shows how the activities could be conducted using similar or equivalent pieces of software. Wherever possible, we have tried to make use of software or internet resources that are freely available, and in some cases we have provided the software needed on the CD-ROM; and we have provided template documents and examples of the sorts of outcomes you may expect from the children on the CD-ROMs for each book. These are in a range of formats to ensure that they are compatible with most programs.

We have assumed most teachers have access to Microsoft Office applications, either on their home computers or the school computers. The majority of educational software will import MS Office software files. If in doubt, consult the manual for the software used in your school to see how, or if, software files can be imported.

You need to decide how the children will access the computer files and templates needed for the project and save their work. If the school has a network, the files needed for the activities could be placed in a folder on the network. Failing this, you may have to install the files on each computer to ensure that the children have access to them. Thorough preparation is the key to success with ICT; never assume that what works on your computer at home will work in the same way on the school computers – always test-run activities on the computers the children will be using.

Planning an ICT project

When planning the projects we drew upon our extensive experience of using ICT in the classroom as primary teachers and as teacher educators. However, we have not called ourselves 'experts'. We have tried to find out what works best for children, teachers and ourselves in real classrooms. It is our opinion that you are the expert concerning what will move your children forward in developing their ICT capabilities. Therefore, we have devised the projects to integrate with a range of subjects in a range of teaching and learning situations. The projects are not intended to be prescriptions or recipes; we expect you to adapt, modify, extend and combine the activities. However, the approach we have used is one that you could readily adopt for your own projects.

A four-stage strategy for developing a project

1. Decide on the destination

Before doing anything else, we decide what the end-result should be, i.e. what ICT learning outcomes the project should produce. In some cases the outcomes could be influenced by the sort of software or hardware we feel is important for the children to experience. Even so, we identify quite clearly what the children will accomplish by the end of the project. It is often quite easy to define the tangible outcome – a multimedia presentation, a video film or a completed database; but is it also important to consider the learning that will be required to enable the children to achieve the outcome.

2. Choose the vehicle that will be used for the journey

At this point you should consider the subject context in which the project will take place. This will have an influence on the next stage of the process, i.e. the route which will be taken. The subject focus could influence the ICT skills which need to be developed. For example, if the destination is the production of a spreadsheet model, the subject context could influence the skills which are needed to produce the model: a spreadsheet model for predicting the distance a toy car travels over different surfaces will need different formulae from one which is used to produce number patterns for mathematics.

3. Determine the route to be taken

There are many journeys which can be taken to reach a destination; hence, it is important to consider the skills, routines, techniques and key ideas which the children ought to accumulate *en route*. For example, if the end-product is to be a representation of an Impressionist painting based on a digital photo, you need to work out what the children need to learn to achieve the result. This will be related to your knowledge of the children's prior experiences, their capabilities and the resources you have available. This aspect can be the most difficult, as you need to scaffold the activities to enable the children to move progressively from one task to the next. Hence, to create their Impressionist picture, the children may need to be taught how Impressionist artists attempted to portray light in their pictures, how to take digital photos, how to use the editing tools in an image-handling program, how to save their work at intervals in case they need to revise what they have done and, finally, how to print out their pictures on good-quality photographic paper.

4. Pack and prepare

Routine everyday journeys need minimal preparation; you get in the car or on the bus and set off. A project is more like a holiday, which may require more careful planning and preparation. Once you have determined the activities in which the children need to participate to acquire the skills and knowledge they need, you should prepare the resources needed to inspire, support and guide them. For example, before expecting the children to edit a video, they will probably need to see an example of the sort of completed video programme that you are intending they should produce. Some activities may require template documents, word banks or bookmarked websites; others may need example files, banks of clipart or data ready for entry. The *Blue Peter* 'Here's one I made earlier' approach is just as relevant for ICT as it is for other practical subjects such as D&T.

This process mirrors that which we went through in writing the projects. You should always be on the lookout for ideas to inspire and enthuse the children. The best ideas are those which others have already tried and found successful – something which underpins the projects in the subject books.

Where to find information, guidance, resources and ideas

This is not an exhaustive list but an overview of the kinds of sources that can inform and inspire your work.

Colleagues

As a teacher, you are probably already in the habit of picking up ideas from other teachers when you call in on their classrooms or visit other schools. The internet provides another means of metaphorically looking over other teachers' shoulders for ideas. Visit teacher websites or browse other schools' websites for ideas.

Teachers' websites

Teachers' websites, such as those listed below, provide a range of resources, from lesson plans to information, software reviews and guidance. Some, such as the Standards website and the Teacher Resource Exchange, include free software downloads of resources for interactive whiteboards, for example.

- The Standards Site – http://www.standards.dfes.gov.uk/
- Becta – http://www.becta.org.uk/
- ICT Advice (provided by Becta) – http://www.ictadvice.org.uk/
- Teachernet – http://www.teachernet.gov.uk/
- Teacher Resource Exchange – http://tre.ngfl.gov.uk/
- Teaching Ideas – http://www.teachingideas.co.uk/
- Primary Resources – http://www.primaryresources.co.uk/
- Schoolzone – http://www.schoolzone.co.uk/
- TEEM (Teachers Evaluating Educational Multimedia) – http://www.teem. org.uk/

These websites are probably the most well known in the field of primary education, but they are not the only ones available. Searching the internet for learning resources, lesson plans or teaching activities will yield many more.

Schools' websites

Most schools have websites, but the following are particularly well known for the resources and ideas they provide, particularly for ICT-based activities:

- Ambleside Primary School – http://www.amblesideprimary.com/

- Sutton-on-Sea Community Primary School – http://www.sutton.lincs.sch.uk/

- Sir Robert Hitcham Primary School – http://www.hitchams.suffolk.sch.uk/

- Woodland Grange Primary School – http://www.woodlandwideweb.org.uk/

Software publishers' websites

Visit the websites of the publishers of the software you use in schools. Most provide free downloads of resources, lesson ideas and additional guidance materials. In addition, many also include trial downloads of their other software titles so that you can try out programs before buying them.

Books, journals and magazines

Since the introduction of ICT into primary schools there has been a continuous stream of publications about ICT. It is not our place to recommend books, but a visit to the Amazon website (www.amazon.co.uk) and a search for 'primary ICT' will provide you with a range of titles that may be useful in giving you information and ideas. Before purchasing the book it might be worthwhile seeing if any reviews have been written about it and/or visiting your local bookshop to browse through it. Some ICT books promise a lot but deliver little.

There are fewer journals devoted to ICT in the primary school than there were ten years ago, but those that are available provide useful ideas and information:

- *Interactive* – an ICT journal aimed at primary teachers – http://www.education-quest.com/main/default.asp

- *Online* – provided as part of the *Times Educational Supplement* every two months and provides information on current events and issues associated with ICT in schools – http://www.tes.co.uk/Online/

- *The Guardian* – includes a monthly supplement about ICT in education – http://education.guardian.co.uk/appleeducation

Conferences, exhibitions and courses

The best-known ICT education conference/exhibition is the BETT (British Educational Technology and Training) show, held in London in January. Virtually every UK supplier of hardware, software and resource materials presents their products and provides ideas and advice. In addition, there are talks and seminars from national figures in the field of educational ICT. The Scottish equivalent (SETT) is usually held in Glasgow in March.

The Education Show, in September, is usually staged at the NEC in Birmingham. Although it is not principally an ICT event, most of the major ICT suppliers have stands.

Your local authority and/or local teacher training providers are bound to run courses in various aspects of ICT. Flyers, posters and information sheets are sent on a regular basis to schools outlining forthcoming training events and courses, though these do not always find their way to the staffroom. Your school's ICT co-ordinator may have information about courses that are currently available.

The children

Do not underestimate the children as a source of ideas, inspiration and guidance. Sometimes an off-hand remark made by a child, or a suggestion might spark off an idea that could turn into a project. For example, one teacher who had just taken delivery of a new digital video camera showed the camera to her Year 1 class and asked them for ideas as to what they could film with it. 'We could do our own cookery TV programme' was one suggestion. This fitted in perfectly with the work the teacher had planned for D&T (and PHSE). The following week the children starred in their own video production, demonstrating how to make gingerbread men. After watching the edited video, they discussed how it could be improved by better presentation and tighter editing. The following week, they planned to make a video on how to make pancakes, with the children doing most of the editing themselves.

References

Ofsted (2004a) Ofsted subject reports 2002/03: *Information and Communication Technology in Primary Schools*. London: Office for Standards in Education.

Ofsted (2004b) 2004 report: *ICT in Schools – The Impact of Government Initiatives: Primary Schools*. London: Office for Standards in Education.

CHAPTER 4

Assessment

[In ICT,] assessment, both formative and summative, continues to be identified as a weakness in many schools. Some schools have introduced assessment frameworks or schemes but in many cases these are not yet in use – or not yet used consistently – by all staff. A combination of helpful written and oral feedback is essential in making formative assessment work.　　(Ofsted 2004: 7)

Why might it be that this overview of all the Ofsted reports for primary schools in 2003/2004 found that teachers were uncertain about how to make assessments of pupils' learning in ICT? Does it mean that:

⊙ teachers are deficient in their knowledge and understanding of teaching ICT?

or might it be that:

⊙ the guidance provided in the National Curriculum for making assessments is vague and imprecise?

⊙ the nature of ICT activities makes assessment difficult?

The purpose of this chapter is to raise awareness of the issues surrounding the assessment of ICT capability and to provide some ideas, strategies and resources for making assessments of pupils' learning when working on ICT activities.

In order to plan for progression it is important that you have an appreciation of where the children are, where they ought to be and where they might be heading next. As John Holt (1969: 82) points out: 'To rescue a man in the woods, you must first know where he is.'

Using the analogy of a journey, as expressed in Chapter 3 on planning for capability, to help a child reach your desired destination you should determine their starting point and then give accurate directions that will enable him/her to plot a course. Assessment, in our view, is the means by which you locate a child's starting point, or their current location, on a continuous journey towards ICT capability.

In Chapter 2 we outlined our interpretation of what constitutes ICT capability – a symbiotic interrelation between skills, routines, techniques, key ideas and independent choice. Because, for us, ICT is inextricably associated with practical outcomes in meaningful subject-related contexts, we are firmly of the belief that the most effective way to assess children's ICT capabilities is by giving them something interesting to do and then monitoring the approaches they use when completing a task.

In our view, most of the key elements of ICT capability are practical. An assessment of finished products will provide only partial and often very limited evidence of a child's ICT capabilities. Routines and techniques, for example, require the combination of a series of sub-skills, some of which are more sophisticated and/or efficient than others. A finished product may not reveal the methods used to complete it. For example, the printout of a document will not show whether the positioning of text has been achieved by the repeated use of the space bar, the use of tab marks, the inclusion of an invisible table or the use of alignment tools (e.g. left, centre or right align). Similarly, unless you know the origins of a piece of internet-based text, you will be uncertain as to the extent to which a child has edited the text or how long and how extensively the child searched for and located relevant pieces of information and/or images (e.g. see *Learning ICT in Science* project 7 – Multimedia information source; *English* project 10 – A *Macbeth* webquest).

Assessing ICT

What assessment methods can be used to capture the application of children's ICT capabilities? The approach we advocate for assessing a pupil's ICT capability is similar to the information-handling cycle used in *Maths* project 6 – Statistical investigations 1 (see Figure 4.1).

Identify what you want the children to learn

Not only have Ofsted inspectors stressed the importance of defining learning objectives for effective teaching; it is also common sense to have a clear idea, at the outset of an activity, of what you want the children to learn.

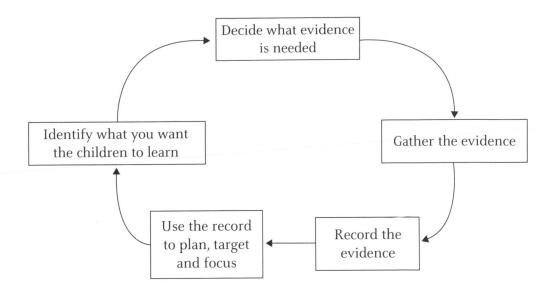

Figure 4.1 The assessment cycle for ICT

In Chapter 2 we identified what we, and others (e.g. Kennewell *et al.* 2000), feel constitutes ICT capability. In Chapter 3 we highlighted the importance of identifying the learning objectives for each activity and sub-task in terms of skills, routines, techniques and key ideas. Take as an example *Learning ICT in English* project 3 – Branching stories. The third activity in this project requires the children to create a page of their story using a word processor. One teacher's learning objectives for this activity might be that, at the end of the activity, the children will achieve the following.

⊙ skills: enter text with a keyboard; embolden headings and the text for button labels

⊙ routines: save their page; print their page

⊙ techniques: import images and position them appropriately for the text; enter, format and edit text to conform with their section of the story

⊙ key ideas: explain how text and images can be used to communicate an episode or event in a story; describe a hyperlink (i.e. how clicking on a button can bring up a new page)

⊙ independent choice: decide which image(s) from a limited selection could best illustrate an event; choose the most appropriate styles for text to convey meaning (e.g. bold to indicate shouting, italic for emphasis).

Another teacher may decide to focus on different learning objectives to address learning needs she has identified or to correspond with the school's specified curriculum.

Decide what evidence is needed

There is often considerable debate among educators about the difference between learning objectives and learning outcomes. Our view is that desired, expected or anticipated outcomes should exemplify the learning they represent, and relate closely to the learning objectives for each activity. For example, the outcome of the branching story activity outlined above (i.e. the page that the children produce) could exemplify the learning objectives as follows:

⊙ skills – expected outcomes demonstrating successful learning will include: relevant text entered from keyboard, including use of space bar, enter key, backspace and shift or caps lock; headings and text for buttons emboldened appropriately

⊙ routines – expected outcomes demonstrating successful learning will include: the page saved successfully to the correct network folder; a file correctly labelled; the page printed successfully

⊙ techniques – expected outcomes demonstrating successful learning will include: images imported and positioned appropriately in the text; text entered, formatted with a range of styles (i.e. bold, italic and indent) to make the story easy to read

⊙ key ideas – expected outcomes demonstrating successful learning will include: clear explanations as to how text and images can be used to communicate an episode or event in a story and reasoned justifications for the layout of their page; an accurate description of a hyperlink (e.g. how pages can be linked by buttons or hotspots)

⊙ independent choice – expected outcomes demonstrating successful learning will include: appropriate image(s) selected for a page; appropriate styles used to convey meaning with explanations as to why the styles have been chosen.

The type of evidence required will be dependent upon the learning objectives for a given activity. In some cases, the content of the text will be important when, for example, a skeleton text has been 'improved' (e.g. *English* project 3 – Branching stories) or the text copied from a web page has been summarised to show key points (e.g. *Humanities* project 8 – Making an information source). At other times the appearance of the text will provide the most significant evidence. Most activities can be adapted to focus on different aspects of learning.

At the planning stage you will need to consider how the children will produce evidence of their learning. If you are trying to assess the extent to which the children can edit text independently for a given purpose, giving them a highly structured writing frame could prevent them from demonstrating this capability. Modifying the task, to one where the children are provided with a skeleton text and/or word bank, could shift the emphasis from entering text to using editing and formatting tools. Children could then concentrate not on the time-consuming task of keying in words but on improving the appearance – and consequently the readability – of their text. Using the same skeleton text as a starting point for all children will provide you with considerable evidence of the differences in your children's capabilities in editing.

Gather the evidence

The approaches that you adopt for gathering the evidence of learning will depend on the type of evidence to be accumulated. Some evidence will be tangible – printed artefacts, on-screen presentations or edited video or sound clips. Other evidence will be more ephemeral, such as the technique used to achieve an effect for a digital image or the search method employed to find a particular website. In an ideal world, the most effective way to gather this less-enduring evidence is continuous observation. While you can do this with very small groups of children, or when a large number of teaching assistants are available, it is less feasible in the usual primary teaching situation.

Some strategies for gathering ephemeral evidence include:

- saving or printing documents at various stages of completion
- asking children to log their decision-making at key points in an activity
- using photographic evidence
- informal observation
- structured observation.

Saving or printing documents at various stages of completion

Not only is it good working practice to save computer-based work at intervals; it can also be a useful way of gathering evidence about the stages a child or pair has gone through in completing a task. For example, the children's concept cartoons

(*Science* project 3) could be saved at intervals with different file names (e.g. rbcart1, rbcart2, etc.). While this approach does not capture specific skills employed, it does provide an indication of the general approach adopted by the children, which can sometimes be quite revealing.

Though less revealing, the children could be encouraged to print out their work at intervals in a lesson to provide evidence of progress. However, this will depend on the type of activity, the school's policy on the use of the printer (particularly if it is a colour printer) and whether the printed evidence will reveal any useful assessment information.

Asking children to log their decision-making at key points in an activity

This could readily be achieved, when working in pairs, by one child completing an activity log sheet explaining the reasoning behind a particular technique or ticking a box to show which approach was selected while the other is working at the keyboard.

A variant of this is to ask the children to self-assess their performance against clear criteria. In a webquest activity (*Learning ICT in English* project 10), for example, the groups check their performance using a criterion grid. See also the Webquest website (www.webquest.org) for more information on drawing up self-assessment criteria.

For younger pupils a simplified self-assessment checklist can be used. On the CD that accompanies each subject book, there is a simple checklist for each project. Children can complete this to indicate how well they thought they had performed against predefined learning objectives. These are presented in Microsoft Word format and can be edited to focus on your own learning objectives. The checklists could be administered after each activity or at particular stages throughout a project to determine progress.

A clear disadvantage of self-assessment is the lack of objectivity. Over-confident children will tend to rate their capabilities more highly than those who are less confident, and sometimes those with more experience are inclined to underrate their performance because they are more aware of what they have still to learn. However, self-assessment provides a useful method of reinforcing for children the purposes of an activity and can help you to triangulate your assessments.

Another factor that needs to be taken into account when making assessments, particularly with ICT, is the level of support that was provided. All the children in a class may produce very similar-looking outcomes, but some may have received substantial guidance and support from you, a support assistant or another child. This needs to be logged when recording the children's responses.

Using photographic evidence

Some activities lend themselves more to the use of photographic evidence – particularly those that have a practical component such as using a programmable toy (*Maths* project 1) or logging data (*Science* project 9).

Another approach is to ask the children to save screenshots of their work at the end of a session or at significant points during an activity. The screenshots can be pasted into a Word document with captions outlining the stages the children went through in completing the task.

Capturing a screenshot

The simplest approach (using a Windows PC) is to press the PRINT SCREEN key (usually situated in the top right corner of the keyboard, sometimes labelled PRT SC). This places a copy of the screen, at the time the key was pressed, onto the computer's clipboard. This can then be pasted into virtually any document:

1. Press the 'PRINT SCREEN' key.
2. Open a new document in your word-processing program (such as MS Word).
3. Paste the screenshot by choosing 'Paste' in the drop-down 'Edit' menu (or right-click and select 'Paste' or hold down the CTRL key and press V).

If you want only a portion of the screen, paste the screenshot into an imaging program such as Paint (available through Programs > Accessories > Paint).

You can amend the image in Paint. (You can also crop the image using the image-handling tools in MS Word.)

The disadvantage to screenshots is that the image captured is saved as a bitmap, which takes up a lot more memory than a compressed alternative such as a JPEG. To save memory, you can paste the screenshot into Paint, save it as a JPEG and then paste it into a Word document. However, this may distract attention from the task in hand, that is logging the children's progress with a task.

Informal observation

When teaching, you make observations about the responses of your children continuously. You monitor the way they respond to your explanations, how they answer your questions, whether they are applying themselves to the tasks you have set, whether you have pitched the level of demand appropriately, and you monitor the changing mood and relationships between different children or groups of children. Much of this information is used to adjust your teaching to cater for the changing needs of the children, unanticipated responses or opportunities to intervene with apposite instructions, explanations or an increase in the level of challenge provided by a task. While the children are engaged with ICT-based activities, informal observations can be used to monitor the ways in which different children respond to an activity. You will notice that some are very confident and can tackle a given task with the minimum of fuss. These children are willing to experiment when they run into problems rather than turning to you for guidance. At the other extreme are children who are reluctant to try anything out for themselves and who persistently seek reassurance that what they are doing is 'right'.

At the end of an ICT lesson, try thinking back to how the children responded to the task. If you have defined clear learning objectives for the activity, as indicated above, then it should be possible to quickly decide who was able to complete the activity with the minimum of support, those who needed considerable support and those who lay somewhere between the two extremes. This information could be logged using a simple coding system (see 'Record the evidence' below). If you have help from a teaching assistant, you could ask for her informal assessment, particularly if she had been supporting a particular group of individuals.

ICT lessons taught in computer suites tend, in most primary schools, to be timetabled on a weekly basis. Logging the children's progress as soon as possible after (or even during) a lesson will provide you with invaluable information about the children's performance to remind you when you come to plan the following week's activities.

Structured observation

Structured observations can be carried out in several ways. You can:

⊙ observe the whole class to gain an overview of its progress

⊙ observe a different group closely each week to gather more detailed information on individual attainment

⊙ target your observations on particular skills.

The main difference between structured and informal observation lies in the preparation. For structured observation you will need a prepared observation schedule which you, or a colleague, complete at intervals during the lesson. You might even prepare a coding system to enable you to log particular responses. For example, assuming you were interested in recording how well the children edited video clips they had shot previously (see *Learning ICT in the Humanities* project 9, *Science* project 8, *English* project 8, *Arts* project 10), the various skills and routines you expect them to use could be coded as:

A – applied with confidence
B – needed some help

C – needed considerable support

D – attempted but unsuccessful

E – not attempted

X – not observed.

It is important that you include the final category (or leave a blank) so that you can identify those children you were unable to observe in a lesson. These children can be prioritised for the next observation. In an ideal world, you should complete the observation schedule during the lesson, while observing the children, but if the children require considerable support during the lesson you may have to complete it retrospectively.

If you have developed a good working relationship with the children you could ask them to complete the schedule on their own performance, and then compare this with your observations.

Record the evidence

In the preceding section we suggested recording structured observations with a schedule. We also suggested logging informal observational data so that ephemeral evidence can be recalled when planning follow-on tasks. This section examines ways in which longer-term records can be used to track children's progress over a year and, where these records are transferred, as a child progresses through a school from class to class.

Ideally, you should know at the start of the year the aspects of learning in ICT that you are intending to cover. If you are using the QCA ICT scheme of work units, these can be extracted from the planning documentation. Alternatively, if you are using the projects in this series, the learning outcomes can be extracted from the chart in Chapter 2 or the Appendix of this book, the project cards in the subject books or the self-evaluation sheets on the relevant CD-ROM. However, as we have already indicated, any project or activity can be adjusted to lay emphasis on particular learning objectives. For example, entering text on a blank screen will provide assessment information on keyboard use. Asking the children to 'improve' a skeleton text will enable you to focus more on the children's use of editing tools and techniques.

Once you have identified the projects or units, spend a little time deciding what particular skills, routines, techniques and key ideas you will emphasise in your teaching and the extent to which you will aim to encourage the application of independent choice.

When this is done, you can construct a recording sheet, which will enable you to plot each child's progress over the year. Remember, there is a difference between merely logging a child's experience (listing what has been covered) and making an assessment as to how well s/he has accomplished a task – hence the importance of a coding system to help record progress.

In Chapter 3 an example was given of how a Year 3 teacher might select a series of projects from the subject books to guide her teaching of ICT for the year:

Autumn term

⊙ *Science* project 3 – Concept cartoons. Linked with the science work on materials and rocks, the children combine text and graphics to portray their understanding of materials and their origins.

⊙ *Maths* project 8 – Modelling investigations. The teacher selects on-line simulation activities that tie in with the numeracy work on measures and the science work on materials.

⊙ *Arts* project 4 – Designing logos. A one-lesson activity related to the children's D&T work on packaging.

Spring term

⊙ *Maths* project 6 – Statistical investigations 1. To support the work in numeracy lessons on data-handling and also work in PE and PHSE on healthy living.

⊙ *English* project 6 – Imaginative e-mail. This project supports the work planned for geography and citizenship and acts as a preliminary to the planned activities for the Summer term on contrasting localities. The school used for the e-mailing project will be used for comparing information about localities.

Summer term

⊙ *Arts* project 6 – Sound pictures. Ties in with planned work for music and for science. Creating, sampling and manipulating sounds.

⊙ *Humanities* project 7 – Link with a contrasting locality. Relates closely to the planned work for geography and builds on the work started in the previous term on e-mail by introducing the children to blogging.

On this basis this teacher could produce the following table (4.1) to chart the children's progress through the activities contained in the projects, using information from the table presented in the Appendix plus some of her own learning objectives to direct the focus for each project.

Using a simple coding system, the teacher is now able to record the children's individual progress through the year. The most frequently used coding system is

Table 4.1 Example of an ICT record-keeping system for a class

Learning objectives	Green group						Red group					
	Adarsh	Samuel	Salsabil	Mary	James	Matthew	Norman	Hadeel	Jessica	Mariha	Jordan	Harshada
Computers use icons to provide information and instructions												
ICT can be used to create pictures to present information												
ICT makes it easy to correct mistakes and explore alternatives												
Format text using bold, italic and alignment												
Import images and use simple drawing tools												
Create and use a spreadsheet model to investigate relationships systematically												
Simulations enable people to investigate 'What if . . . ?' situations												
Import clipart into a spreadsheet												
How information is presented in a spreadsheet in cells which can be interrelated												
How formulae can be used to interrelate cells												
Copy and paste parts of a 'painting'												
Pictures can be assembled by repeating elements												
Change colours and evaluate choices												
Making marks on the screen using 'undo' makes it easy to correct mistakes and explore alternatives												
A screen image can be a finished product												
Images can be created by combining and manipulating objects												
Search for records which meet particular criteria in a database												

Table 4.1 (continued)

Learning objectives	Green group						Red group					
	Adarsh	Samuel	Salsabil	Mary	James	Matthew	Norman	Hadeel	Jessica	Mariha	Jordan	Harshada
Present information as bar charts in a database												
Create a simple database												
Transfer a chart/graph as an image from a database to a word-processed document												
How databases are structured to resemble an electronic card index system												
Write and respond to e-mails												
Add and open attach-ments to e-mails												
It is very important to protect your identity when using the internet												
Some people who use the internet pretend to be someone else												
Select skills and techniques to organise, reorganise and communicate ideas												
Electronic and live sounds can be combined in a perform-ance												
ICT can be used to record and manipulate sounds to develop and refine a musical composition												
Sounds can be stored as computer files												
ICT can be used to exchange information in text and image form												
Web applications can be used to facilitate a dialogue between users in different locations												
An awareness of audience is important when communicating using the internet												

one that is extensible – as the children make progress the symbols can be changed to indicate how their knowledge and skills are growing. The simplest coding is the use of multiple ticks:

✓ indicates some grasp but in need of further reinforcement

✓✓ indicates a basic grasp of the skill, knowledge or concept

✓✓✓ indicates a sound grasp.

Some teachers favour a triangular notation, signifying the same levels as above (see Figure 4.2).

Figure 4.2 Example of a notation system

Whatever system you decide to adopt, one that allows you to revise your initial judgements not only saves effort (by enabling you to re-use your assessment record) but also encourages effective and efficient assessment practices (you can focus your attention on children needing to be reassessed).

Use the record to plan, target and focus

In the above example the teacher has planned to include a running theme (the manipulation of images) through the projects. She is therefore able to use her assessment records to re-focus her teaching in subsequent activities. If, for example, she finds that after the initial project most of the children are highly confident in manipulating images, she can adjust the activities in the arts project to provide the children with more challenge. If she finds there is a group that needs extra support, she can ensure that her teaching or the attention of a teaching assistant is directed to this in subsequent project activities. If she finds she has over-estimated the capabilities of the children, in her next project she can scaffold the tasks more carefully to provide more opportunities to build the children's skills and develop routines and techniques.

Identifying clear objectives not only helps you to target your assessments and ensure you are planning for progression, but also helps you to structure your assessment opportunities. For example, it has already been mentioned that skills, routines and techniques are more difficult to assess than the children's grasp of key ideas – primarily because they require careful observation to make judgements on the approaches used by the children to complete the tasks. It is unrealistic to expect that you will be able to observe every child for a sufficient length of time in each ICT lesson to make an assessment of every technique that he or she is using. However, by carefully logging the children's progress through a project, you will be able to target your observations in each lesson. By the end of a project you will, ideally, have had an opportunity to make informal and maybe structured observations of every child or group at least once.

Issues associated with assessing ICT

Previously, we highlighted one issue affecting the assessment of ICT – as ICT is a practical subject it is often difficult to gather ephemeral evidence of the children's responses to tasks and activities. Other issues you will need to consider and address are:

- there is sometimes a conflict between ICT objectives and subject learning
- children often work in pairs at the computer
- technical problems sometimes affect children's work
- children with computers at home are at an advantage
- it is sometimes difficult to decide what the child has done and what the computer has done for him/her.

There is sometimes a conflict between ICT objectives and subject learning

It is inevitable that, at times, the learning objectives for the subject take precedence over those for ICT. For example, if the children are editing a skeleton text or embellishing a brainstormed word list to write a poem, your key focus might be on the quality of the children's writing rather than the editing techniques that have been used. The ultimate aim in developing children's ICT capability is to make the technology 'transparent' – the children become so focused on using ICT as a tool to achieve other outcomes that they hardly notice that they are using technology itself. For example, when you are writing something with a word processor, you probably do not need to search the keyboard for the relevant key – you have passed that stage. You may even be completely unaware of the keyboard as you frame your sentences.

When you mistype a word do you:

- use backspace to erase it and retype it as you write?

- right-click on the word and use the spelling options offered?

- use the spell-check facility on your computer to check the whole document after you have typed it?

- correct each mistake by hand after finishing the document?

The chances are that you will use a combination of these techniques. Your choice will be dependent on the nature of the task, whether you touch-type or watch the keyboard while you are typing, the pressures of time, your skills with the keyboard, your experience, and so on. For example, if you have never realised (or been told) that you can right-click on a spelling error in Word to see the suggested spelling options, you will probably never have used this function. The majority of us have acquired our word-processing techniques through trial and improvement, by occasionally reading the manual or by accessing on-screen help or asking a friend.

Similarly, you have probably reached the stage where you do not think twice about saving a document, or using Google (or something similar) to search the internet. You have developed a range of 'transparent' routines and techniques that are part of your unconscious action. This is the goal all primary teachers should be aiming to achieve for their pupils – equipping the children with sufficient experience to enable them to use ICT without having to stop and think.

Most of us learn ICT skills on a need-to-know basis. We may be aware that MS Word can produce an index for us, but will only ever use it if we have to write a dissertation or a book. It is our view that the most effective way of teaching children ICT skills and techniques is to create a need, and then to be on hand to show them what to do when they are engaged in the problem.

We have stressed the importance of developing children's abilities and confidence to make independent choices. As the children progress through the primary school it will be inevitable that the focus will shift away from the development of low-level skills and routines. The children will be improving or extending the range of techniques they use. The focus in the subject books is on providing the children with meaningful subject-related contexts, to help them forget that they are using a computer to achieve their goals. It is not only inevitable that the subject learning objectives will ultimately overshadow those for ICT, it is essential that they should. However, as a teacher you should be constantly monitoring the way the children are solving the problems and doing the tasks so that you are able to show them new or more efficient methods of using ICT to achieve the learning outcomes.

We believe that 'proficiency increases efficiency'.

Children often work in pairs at the computer

In even the best-equipped primary schools children tend to work in pairs at the computer. It has been argued (e.g. McFarlane 1997) that computer-based activities actually promote collaborative work more than any other classroom activities. The screen is more public than a page of writing and there is a natural tendency for children to discuss and share what they are doing on a computer. It may have something to do with watching television, which is usually a shared experience.

However, some pairings lead to an unequal sharing of responsibility or effort. Inevitably, there are keyboard-hoggers who seldom allow their partner access to the computer, and there are those who are more than happy to sit back and let their partner do the work for them. There are also those who lack confidence or experience and are afraid to expose their perceived inadequacy to public scrutiny (and possible ridicule). Much of this depends on the social climate that is engendered in the school or an individual classroom. In classrooms where there is a mutually supportive atmosphere, children are more likely to help and support each other.

While you can take into account the possible influence of pairings when making assessments of individual performance, you can also use some strategies to make sure that both children have an equal opportunity to contribute to an activity. In addition to trying to change the climate of co-operation that exists in the classroom, you can use other ICT-specific approaches to overcome some of the difficulties of paired work:

⊙ give the children specific roles or tasks when engaged in an activity

⊙ signal changeovers regularly during a lesson to ensure the pairs get equal access to the keyboard

⊙ train the children in paired working

⊙ prepare on-computer and off-computer tasks during an ICT lesson.

Give the children specific roles or tasks when engaged in an activity

Some activities lend themselves to the allocation of roles. The most obvious example is the webquest (e.g. *Learning ICT in English* project 10 – *Macbeth* webquest). The original concept of the webquest assumed the children would work in teams to complete the allotted tasks and that each member of the team would be allocated a specific role. In the *Macbeth* webquest, for example, the children are required to present a proposal to a film company for their re-interpretation of Shakespeare's story. The costume designer searches for information on appropriate costumes, the location manager looks for locations, the director plans the scenes, and so on. A similar approach can be adopted for most ICT-based activities. For example, when shooting a video, someone could be allocated the role of camera operator, others could be actors, etc.

When children are working in pairs on a computer-based activity, it may be more difficult to assign roles unless the activity has quite specific components. For example, *Humanities* project 8 – Making an information source – requires the children to search for information on the internet and then re-present it using multimedia. One child could be responsible for locating and downloading the information (the researcher) while the other could be responsible for creating the presentation (the presenter). The partner who is not working on the keyboard could be recording the progress of the activity on a logging sheet; then they can switch roles.

Signal changeovers regularly during a lesson to ensure the pairs get equal access to the keyboard

An approach more suited to younger children is to signal clearly to the children when it is time to change over. If you are using an approach to teaching new skills where the activity has been 'chunked' into sub-tasks, the pairs could alternate when completing each sub-task. If the activity is more continuous, you could announce when the changeover should occur arbitrarily. Children who are used to working co-operatively may only need to be reminded to change roles regularly during the lesson. However, you should keep monitoring the children to ensure that the pairs are sharing equally.

Train the children in paired working

In the subject books we sometimes suggest that inexperienced children could be supported through peer tutoring. If this approach is adopted it is essential that the children be well briefed on their roles. For example, a more experienced child should be taught how to guide the other by explanation rather than demonstration. How many times have you been in the position where a more confident computer user has quickly shown you how to do something and then left you to fumble about trying to recall which keys were pressed and which menus were accessed?

In *Learning ICT in English* project 3 – Branching stories – information is provided on supporting the development of children's exploratory talk. This involves giving the children clear rules about how they should take account of all others' contributions and ideas before making a decision. Similarly, you could encourage the children to suggest, agree to and then abide by a set of rules they will follow when working at the computer. For example:

⊙ ask your partner if s/he would like to use the keyboard before using it

⊙ ask your partner for his/her ideas before typing something

73

⊙ never use the keyboard for more than five minutes before letting your partner use it.

Prepare on- and off-computer tasks during an ICT lesson

Another way to ensure that both children in a pair get equal access to the computer is to provide an off-computer task that runs alongside the computer-based task. For example, in *Science* project 10 – Using search engines – once text has been printed off from a website, one child could annotate the printout to show how it could be edited for their presentation.

This approach is easier if the computers are classroom-based or if the school's computer suite has tables at which the children can work. Alternatively, if two adults are available, half the class could be working in the computer suite while the other children are working on the paper-based task in the classroom.

Technical problems sometimes affect children's work

The most common problem encountered in school is being unable to print out the children's work once it has been completed. In these circumstances an assessment of the children's work can be made using observations and what can be seen on screen.

The most difficult technical problem to overcome is the loss of the children's work through a computer crash or a corrupted file. While this can never be predicted, you should always assume the worst and encourage children to save their work as it progresses to ensure that they always have a previous version they can return to. Sometimes it is possible to recover a lost document; *Textease*, for example, will usually recover a document automatically, provided the program is restarted immediately after it crashes. If you have the help of a computer technician (some schools share one), you could ask him/her to see if a deleted or corrupted file is recoverable.

Children with computers at home are at an advantage

This will generally become apparent after working with the children for a short while. Some children will ask if they can continue working on ICT activities for homework. Just as some parents are more supportive than others, this should not be discouraged.

Some schools try to compensate for other children's lack of access to computers outside school by running after-school computer clubs. In some schools, computer clubs and classes are provided for parents as well as for children.

In terms of assessment, it can sometimes be difficult to determine the extent to which a child has had help from a parent or sibling. In these circumstances, you could always ask the child to demonstrate the methods s/he used to complete an activity.

It is sometimes difficult to decide what the child has done and what the computer has done for him/her

In addition to making observations, you can tackle this issue by talking to the children or asking older children to write a reflective report about the approach they used to complete a project. The CD-ROM accompanying each of the subject books includes a self-assessment sheet for each project that encourages the children to reflect on the extent to which they have developed new knowledge and skills. These could be used as the basis for discussions or more comprehensive reflective commentaries on the approaches they used.

A plenary 'show and tell' session will provide an opportunity for the children to explain or demonstrate routines or techniques they have developed or discovered. Indeed, encouraging the children to experiment and devise novel approaches is an important part of developing their capabilities of becoming independent, confident users of ICT.

Working with the projects

Interpreting National Curriculum level descriptions

As mentioned in the introduction to this chapter, one of the difficulties teachers have with making assessments of children's progress in ICT is the National Curriculum level descriptions. Because these have been written to be applicable to a variety of possible learning outcomes, they are highly generalised and hence open to a wide range of interpretation.

The projects in the subject books include information on the National Curriculum levels of attainment they address. Provided the children work successfully through the activities, the outcome of their work ought to fall within the range of levels shown on the project fact card. For example, *Arts* project 5 – Digital photos – has been written to provide children with opportunities to produce work that demonstrates capabilities at levels 2 to 3. It can be assumed, therefore, that if a child is unable to complete the activities, he/she is not working at level 2 (either level 1 or below). Those whose work just achieves the outcomes for the project can be assumed to be working at level 2, while those who achieve the outcomes comfortably could be working at level 3.

Every project includes information about how it can be adjusted for those who need extra support or additional challenge. In the example above, if the level of challenge were raised, it could be assumed that the children would be working towards, or at, level 4.

For further information on making level-related assessments of children's work (not only in ICT), refer to the National Curriculum in Action website (www. ncaction.org.uk). This site provides detailed guidance on making judgements of children's attainment and annotated examples of children's work that you can use to compare with your children's work.

Certificates

Included on each CD-ROM accompanying the subject books are certificates that can be given to the children on completion of each project. These are provided in MS Word format to enable you to make amendments should you wish to modify the projects in the books. There are two versions of the certificate for each project – a completion certificate and a merit certificate, which could be given to those children you feel deserve particular mention. It is well documented that some children who find conventional schoolwork difficult excel when using a computer. Giving 'public' recognition of achievement to such children could provide them with a boost to their self-esteem.

Figure 4.3 Example of a merit certificate from *Learning ICT in English*

Evaluation sheets

Also included on the CD-ROM with each book are self-evaluation sheets that the children complete at the end of each project. These serve a dual purpose of reminding the children of the learning objectives for the project while providing you with some additional evidence of the children's progress.

The sheets ask the children to indicate their levels of knowledge and skill before and after completing the project. The drawbacks of using self-assessment sheets

How much I have learned?

Name: _____   **Date:**   1 April 2006

Knowledge	How much I knew before the project Nothing · · · A lot	How much I now know after the project Nothing · · · A lot
What an e-mail address looks like	☐ ☐ ☐ ☐	☐ ☐ ☐ ☐
What an attachment is	☐ ☐ ☐ ☐	☐ ☐ ☐ ☐
The rules for safe use of e-mail	☐ ☐ ☐ ☐	☐ ☐ ☐ ☐
The rules for exploratory talk	☐ ☐ ☐ ☐	☐ ☐ ☐ ☐

Comments
The most interesting thing I learned was:

Skills	How well I could do it before the project Not at all · · · Very well	How well I can do it after the project Not at all · · · Very well
How to send an e-mail	☐ ☐ ☐ ☐	☐ ☐ ☐ ☐
How to open an e-mail	☐ ☐ ☐ ☐	☐ ☐ ☐ ☐
How to reply to an e-mail	☐ ☐ ☐ ☐	☐ ☐ ☐ ☐
How to attach a document to an e-mail	☐ ☐ ☐ ☐	☐ ☐ ☐ ☐
How to use editing tools in a word processor	☐ ☐ ☐ ☐	☐ ☐ ☐ ☐

Comments
The most useful skill I learned was:

Figure 4.4 Example of a self-assessment sheet from *Learning ICT in English* project 6

such as these have been discussed previously in this chapter, but most primary teachers are fully aware of those children who have an unrealistic view of their own capabilities. These sheets are useful in helping you triangulate your assessments, alerting you to issues of which you may be unaware and helping to indicate those children who have decided the project has enabled them to make significant progress. Formalising learning for the children in this way helps the children to appreciate the purpose of the activities they complete in school and alert them to ways in which they could enhance their learning.

Summary

In this chapter we have explored some of the issues associated with making assessments of children's ICT capabilities and proffered some solutions. We have emphasised the importance of defining clear learning objectives for ICT activities and determining the outcomes which will demonstrate learning. We have provided some suggestions on how ephemeral evidence can be gathered and how assessments can be recorded, using an extensible coding system to ensure that records can be used progressively through a project.

As the children progress through the primary school the emphasis will shift from assessing low-level skills and routines to making judgements about the techniques employed and the levels of independent choice being shown. The ultimate aim for the primary teacher is to enable the children to reach the stage where the technology they are using becomes sufficiently 'transparent' that they are almost unaware of its existence.

References

Holt, J. (1969) *How Children Fail*. London: Penguin.

Kennewell S., Parkinson, J. and Tanner, H. (2000) *Developing the ICT Capable School*. London: RoutledgeFalmer.

McFarlane, A. (1997) 'Thinking about writing', in McFarlane, A. (ed.) *Information Technology and Authentic Learning*. London: RoutledgeFalmer.

Ofsted (2004) Report: *ICT in Schools: The Impact of Government Initiatives: Primary Schools*. London: Office for Standards in Education.

CHAPTER 5

Organising and managing ICT

The principal purpose of this chapter is to examine the issues associated with organising and managing ICT resources and activities in the primary school and to put forward ideas and suggestions for maximising resources and time.

One of the greatest virtues of ICT is its flexibility and hence its capacity for increasing the efficiency of teaching and learning by combining the development of ICT capabilities with children's subject learning. However, to gain these benefits you need to carefully plan the opportunities provided for children to use ICT resources and organise the equipment, materials, time, children and adult support. These issues are explored in this chapter and suggestions are made for a range of organisational approaches drawing upon the writers' extensive experience, and case studies exemplifying effective strategies.

This chapter draws upon the principles and practices that underpin the educational approaches on which this series of books is founded. The guiding principles are detailed in Chapter 1.

The classroom computer

In primary schools, computers tended, formerly, to be primarily classroom-based. Increased funding for ICT has prompted many schools to create computer suites or shared computer areas. Some have decided to retain classroom-based computers, either for pragmatic reasons (e.g. insufficient space) or because this organisation accords with the school's educational philosophy, such thinking being particularly prevalent in early years' settings. Some schools have opted for a compromise; classroom computer(s) or wireless, networked laptops and a suite.

The great advantage of having one or more classroom computers is accessibility – you and the children can use a computer that is most appropriate for the task in hand. For example, if a child needs an obscure piece of information, she can immediately search the internet (e.g. *Learning ICT in Science* project 10), or a pair of children can develop their response to a classroom activity with a multimedia presentation (see *Humanities* project 5, *Science* project 7, *English* project 4). Similarly, relevant or long-term investigations or experiments can be conducted in front of children, such as a time-lapse movie of seed germination with a digital microscope (*Science* project 2) or data-logging (*Science* project 9). Another positive advantage of having a classroom computer is to support teaching, particularly if the classroom is equipped with a data projector, plasma screen display or interactive whiteboard (see below for information on interactive whiteboards and alternatives).

A disadvantage of classroom-based computers for supporting learning is their management and organisation; they are insufficient in number for all children in the class to work on ICT tasks simultaneously. While this could be regarded as a problem by some, it can become an asset in some circumstances. Take, for example, *English* project 3 – Branching stories. If this project is conducted in a computer suite the pairs of children will probably begin the process of writing their section of the story at the same time. This will cause few problems if they all finish their writing and illustrations together, but inevitably some will complete their work within one lesson while others may require two or even three lessons. While extension activities can be prepared for those who finish early, it is probable that compromises will be made to accommodate the slower workers – their sections will be incomplete or underdeveloped.

If, however, the same project is carried out on one or more classroom computers, some sort of rota system will enable the pairs to work in turn on their sections. Pairs will have the benefit of seeing preceding sections and can thereby ensure that their contribution ties in more closely with the developing narrative. In theory, each pair can take whatever amount of time they feel is necessary to write their section. In practice, however, there will be an overall time limit on the completion of the project which will dictate the average length of time that each pair has access to the computer.

Probably the most effective solution for this type of project is to combine the suite with the classroom computer(s). Those who need extra time to complete their work can be accommodated as they and the classroom computers become available.

When managing a classroom computer the following points need to be considered:

⊙ where the computer will be located

⊙ what software will be installed

⊙ how and when the children will use it

⊙ who will maintain and manage the computer.

Location

It might well be that there is only one feasible position for the computer in your classroom, but the following questions may help you to decide whether another position would improve the way it is used.

Where are the sockets?

This will often dictate the location of the computer unless you are using wireless laptops (see below). While both mains and network cables can be extended, for health and safety reasons it is not advisable to run leads across doorways or other thoroughfares. If the school has wireless access to the network, it is possible for any computer to have a wireless network card installed instead of using a network cable. This might enable you to move the computer to another part of the classroom to address some of the other issues listed below.

You should also consider other health and safety issues such as ensuring that the computer is well away from water and that it is unlikely to be knocked over or jolted by an opening door.

Does the screen reflect unwanted light?

Positioning the screen opposite a source of light or in direct sunlight is not only uncomfortable for the user but it can also make viewing what is on the screen difficult.

Is the computer going to distract other children?

Visually stimulating images and animations can have a mesmerising effect on some children, who may decide that what is on the computer looks far more interesting than their allocated desk-based tasks. Similarly, you should decide whether to equip the computer with headphones, maybe with a splitter-lead to allow two sets of headphones to be connected to the computer's single headphone socket.

Is the furniture appropriate?

Furniture that has been specifically designed for computer use in the classroom should take account of the ergonomic needs of the children. The chairs that the children use while at the computer ought to be adjustable to accommodate their different heights. As a rough guide, the monitor should be at eye level, the keyboard at elbow level and the children's feet should rest on the floor or on a footrest when they are seated.

Software

What ICT activities will the children be doing?

The children will need to access the software required for ICT tasks planned for the class for that academic year. The software you choose will depend upon the school's long-term planning for the year group in question, the appropriateness of the software for the age-group, and your own preferences, as a teacher, for favoured programs. You may prefer one specific database package or have a favourite educational word processor. Your choices will be constrained by the need for continuity in the children's experiences as they progress through the school, and also by what is available.

You will also probably need general reference tools and generic software such as an electronic dictionary, CD-ROM encyclopaedia, a painting or photo-editing package and, of course, a web browser for accessing the internet. You might also want to include some basic drill and practice programs for spelling or basic number-knowledge development.

Do you have the relevant licences to install the software?

Some programs are purchased with a site licence, which permits installation on all the computers in the school; other licences allow installation of the software on a specific number of computers at any one time. You may find that some programs are restricted to 'single user' installation, which means you can only install them on one computer per installation disk. For example, some talking stories and encyclopaedias will only work if the CD is present in the disk drive. Other programs may run without the CD being present but are, nevertheless, for a single user. To prevent possible prosecution by software companies you should check the licensing arrangements for your school's software before assuming that you can install it freely on your classroom computer. (It is illegal to copy commercial software or to 'borrow' programs from colleagues in other schools without the permission of the software company.)

The internet provides us with a rich source of open source software and freeware. These are programs that can be installed freely on any number of computers. The CDs that accompany the project books in this series include information and links to examples of such software, relevant to the activities described in the projects. For example, the arts project on digital photos (*Arts* project 5) describes how the activities can be completed using a free photo-editing program called *PhotoFiltre*.

How and when will the children use the computer?

Will you use a rota system?

Theoretically, there is enough time for every child in the class, working with a partner, to have an hour's hands-on experience with one classroom computer, even when assembly time and PE lessons are excluded. However, children who are working on the computer will be unable to participate in whole-class activities and plenaries when these coincide with their allocated ICT time-slot. There may be occasions when you feel justified in allowing the ICT rota to override other classroom activities to ensure that a project is completed within a particular timescale.

If you have a classroom computer you will have to take a professional decision as to whether, how or when your computer rota will take precedence over other classroom activities – is participation required by every child in every whole-class activity every day, or can a pair miss one during a week?

Will they use it as a continuous resource?

In much the same way as you would set organisational procedures for children to make use of classroom resources such as dictionaries, calculators, coloured pencils, erasers and writing-paper, you should decide how the children will make use of computer-based resources such as the internet, electronic dictionaries, spell-checkers or encyclopaedias. For example, at the start of every literacy lesson it may be one child's responsibility to load a dictionary or thesaurus program for use by a target group.

Will it be used for teaching?

If the main use of the computer is for teaching (for example, if it is connected to an interactive whiteboard), you will have less flexibility in the computer's deployment for use by children. It could be argued that using the classroom computer solely for your own use is a waste of a valuable resource. There will be occasions when the computer is not required for teaching purposes and could therefore be made available for use by children to, for example, complete unfinished ICT work or to access reference material (as in the suggested classroom activities outlined earlier). It may even be possible to use a rolling rota whereby the next pair of children on the list will be able to use the computer for completion of work or an ongoing activity when their turn arises.

Who will maintain and manage the computer?

Who will replenish consumables?

Assuming the computer is attached to a printer, some procedures will be required for replenishing the paper and for replacing expended ink cartridges. Children could be shown how to add more paper but you or a colleague should be responsible for changing cartridges.

Alternatively, if your classroom computer is connected to the school network, it should be possible for printing to be done on a central networked printer maintained by a technician or the ICT co-ordinator.

How and where will the children save their work?

The most efficient strategy for saving work is for children to be allocated a folder for their documents on the school's Virtual Learning Environment (VLE) or network. Thus, whenever and wherever they log on to a computer, every child will be able to load previously saved work and save files. If this is not feasible, but you have access to the internet, it is possible to create individual log-ins for you and the children on data-storage websites such as www.freewebspace.net. This will also enable them to access their work from home, assuming they are connected to the internet.

If your classroom computer is not linked to the network or the internet, the children could save their work to their own named folder in 'My Documents' on the computer's built-in hard-disk drive. A system such as RM *Window Box* or *WinSuite* will provide a tailored working environment ensuring that the children cannot accidentally save their work in obscure locations or delete other children's files.

Another, less attractive, option is for the children to be allocated their own floppy disks for saving their work. Not only will the children need to be carefully instructed in how to save and load their work, but you will also have to devise a storage system for their disks. You will also discover that many of the more interesting and exciting projects that take advantage of today's computers' increased memory and advanced graphical features, such as audio-editing (e.g. *Learning ICT in English* project 4, *Arts* project 6), manipulating digital images (e.g. *Arts* project 5, *English* project 7), multimedia (*Humanities* project 8, *Science* project 7, *English* project 9), and editing digital video (e.g. *English* project 8, *Science* project 8, *Humanities* project 9), cannot be saved to a floppy disk owing to the limited capacity of the disks. Furthermore, many modern computers do not now include floppy-disk drives.

It is possible for children to save their work to memory-sticks or burn their work to CD, but these options are also less attractive because of the cost of the former and the lack of flexibility with the latter.

Who will start up and shut down the computer?

While very young children can be shown how to start up and close down computers, it is advisable for an adult to be responsible for these tasks to ensure that they are done properly, thereby avoiding potentially damaging technical problems. Older children could take over these responsibilities provided they are well briefed. If you are new to a school, it is advisable to check what procedures are in place for logging on, logging out and closing down the computers.

What system will you use for introducing new skills and handling software problems?

Some teachers find that appointing computer monitors (children with responsibility for sorting out minor technical problems) relieves the burden of having to continually be on call when the computer is being used. The monitors could also assist when children need briefing about a new task. Alternatively, the outgoing pair on the rota could brief the incoming pair on the task and reinforce their own learning by passing on their skills and explaining techniques.

The interactive whiteboard

Interactive whiteboards (IWBs) provide the means for projecting the computer screen and detecting the position of a stylus or, in the case of a touch-sensitive IWB such as a *Smartboard*, a finger on the board. One of the greatest virtues of an IWB is the ease with which the teacher can present information and activities matched to the changing needs of the class when engaged in whole-class interactive teaching. For example, if you were using a whiteboard activity to introduce the children to the concept of 'take away', when teaching subtraction, and a child explained his method using 'counting back', you could immediately access a different presentation showing 'counting back'. While this might be possible using conventional maths apparatus, the IWB can be used more flexibly and can emphasise differences and similarities in the techniques more readily – provided you have the resources and a well-organised system for locating them on your computer.

Accumulating resources for interactive whiteboard teaching

Increasingly, software companies are producing educational programs and resources specifically designed for use with interactive whiteboards. We have provided some resources on the CDs accompanying the subject books in this series. In addition, the greatest source of materials for use with an IWB is the internet. These resources can be categorised as:

⊙ downloadable resources produced by teachers

⊙ commercially produced downloadable resources

⊙ on-line resources.

Downloadable resources produced by teachers

Most of the resources presented on the web are produced by teachers who wish to share their efforts with the rest of the profession. These vary in quality and may take up a considerable amount of time in searching for ideas that will enhance teaching. The advantage of teacher-produced resources are that, in the main, they are adaptable, as they have been developed with familiar programs such as *PowerPoint, Textease* or the presentation tools provided with the IWB (e.g. *Notebook* (Smart), *Flipchart* (Promethean)).

The most reliable source of materials produced by teachers is the Teacher Resource Exchange (www.tre.ngfl.gov.uk), managed by the National Grid for Learning (NGfL). Other sources of teacher-produced materials include Topmarks (www.topmarks.co.uk), Primary Resources (www.primaryresources.co.uk), Teaching Resources (www.teaching-resources.co.uk), Click Teaching (www.clickteaching.com) and Teaching Ideas (www.teachingideas.co.uk). There are, of course, many others based in this country and in the US.

Commercially produced downloadable resources

Downloadable resources have an advantage over on-line resources in that once they have been downloaded to your computer you can continue to use them. Sometimes on-line resources are removed and therefore are no longer available for use. Some of the projects in the subject books make use of downloadable resources and games. For example, *Learning ICT in Maths* project 8 – Modelling investigations – makes use of *Duck Builder* (downloadable from www.cgpbooks.co.uk). All the on-line and downloadable resources used in the projects are listed in the books, and live links to the relevant websites are included on the accompanying CD-ROMs.

Shareware websites, such as TuCows (www.tucows.com) and Shareware.com (www.shareware.com), provide access to large numbers of programs that can be downloaded and used on your computer. Searching the databases for relevant educational programs usually yields a fair selection, though the quality is variable. Some shareware websites are provided specifically for software appropriate for children, such as *Kids Domain* (www.kidsdomain.com) and on *Linkup Parents* (www.linkup-parents.com). Shareware programs can be downloaded and installed but include some restrictions on usage until a small fee is paid to register and gain access to the full features. Freeware and open source software, on the other hand, is not restricted and can be installed and used on any computer. A useful source of freeware is Freewarehome.com.

On-line resources

On-line resources for teaching and learning abound on the internet. Some are available only by paying an annual subscription (e.g. *Espresso, BigBus*) while others can be accessed free of charge. Regional Broadband Consortia (RBCs), such as the Birmingham Grid for Learning (BGfL) (www.bglf.org), have commissioned the development of on-line resources appropriate for use with interactive whiteboards. BGfL has, for example, developed a series of dedicated resources and provides links to a large number of other freely accessible resources. Probably the most comprehensive range of freely accessible on-line educational resources is provided on the BBC website (www.bbc.co.uk/schools). Other TV companies offer similar resources, and a few evenings browsing the internet will provide you with a range of other sources.

Links to a range of relevant on-line resources are provided in the subject books and on the CD-ROMs in this series. For example, *Humanities* project 1 – Decision-making with a mouse – makes use of the Geographical Association's web resources for children, and *English* project 3 – Branching stories – suggests that use can be made of on-line stories such as *Adventure Island* (kotn.ntu.ac.uk).

Alternatives to an interactive whiteboard

The educational advantages of IWBs have been widely aired. The British Education and Communications Technology Agency (Becta) suggests that the key benefits of IWBS are that they:

- encourage more varied, creative and seamless use of teaching materials
- engage students to a greater extent than conventional whole-class teaching, increasing enjoyment and motivation
- facilitate student participation through the ability to interact with materials on the board.

However, all these benefits can be achieved without the need for investment in quite expensive technology. The greatest virtue of an IWB is the ability to project the computer screen so that it is visible to all the children in the class. This requires the use of a data projector or can be accomplished with a very large monitor or plasma screen. It is not necessary to buy an IWB if the main objective is for children to be able to view the screen.

The second most useful feature of an IWB is the ability to control the mouse pointer by touching the whiteboard with either a stylus or a finger. Remote control of the mouse pointer can be achieved in other ways, which are considerably less expensive. The most cost-effective method is through the purchase of a wireless mouse and keyboard. These can be passed around the class, enabling the children to control the mouse pointer and/or type in text without leaving their seats.

This has the added advantage of preventing children from standing in the potentially eye-damaging beam of the projector lamp and also prevents them from obscuring the view of the rest of the class. Another method of controlling the mouse pointer is by making use of a wireless graphics tablet or a tablet PC. The mouse pointer is moved by 'drawing' on the tablet or the computer screen with a stylus. Again, the children do not need to leave their seats to control the pointer on the screen. Finally, an 'air mouse' can be used to control the mouse pointer on screen. The pointer follows the movements of the mouse as it is moved through the air.

Laptops

Wireless laptop computers are making a considerable impact on the way ICT activities can be incorporated into primary lessons. A class set of laptops can be wheeled from class to class in a specially constructed trolley that will recharge the laptops' batteries when stored. Some trolleys include a wireless transmitter so that the school's existing wired network can be used with the laptops within the classroom.

The flexibility that wireless laptops add to teaching in the classroom is obvious:

⊙ ICT activities can be integrated readily into class work

⊙ the computers can be used when they are most appropriate for the work involved

⊙ the computers can be used anywhere in the room without the need for trailing wires

⊙ internet and networked software can be accessed anywhere, anytime.

The computer is perceived as a flexible tool to assist with whatever task is being addressed and can therefore be integrated more readily into subject teaching.

In terms of organisation and management, the most significant issue is that of battery life. Although the running time on battery power for laptop computers is increasing as battery technology improves and the efficiency of laptops increases, the average length of time a laptop can be used between recharges is presently two to three hours. Discharging the battery completely before recharging will help to prolong its life, but the time between charges will deteriorate over time as the battery becomes less efficient.

It is rarely possible to use a laptop computer for a whole day, unless it can be used on mains power at some point. This will clearly have an impact on the way the taught sessions are organised. For example, because a set of school laptops can only be used for half of each day, it will be difficult to ensure all classes in a school have access during the space of a week.

Solutions to the problem of battery life include:

⊙ providing the laptops with replacement batteries that can be changed over at midday

⊙ ensuring the laptops are configured for optimum battery usage

⊙ organising the teaching sessions so that there are opportunities for battery top-ups

⊙ encouraging the children to adopt battery-efficient behaviours (e.g. switching to stand-by whenever they are not using the computer, avoiding the use of CD-ROM-based programs, making minimal use of wireless features)

⊙ ensuring that the laptops purchased have the longest possible battery running time (this is usually listed in the manufacturer's specification). Generally, the cheapest laptops have the shortest battery running times.

The organisation of the laptops within the classroom will largely depend on the uses to which they are put. However, you can apply a few general principles:

⊙ Ensure the laptops are prepared for use before the lesson. This might mean loading the files the children will be using onto the computer's hard drive or checking that the resources they will need are accessible through the wireless network. Not only will this preparation help with the smooth running of the lesson, but it could also save battery power.

⊙ Devise a management system for the deployment and return of the laptops. For example, set up a rota system or target usage to particular groups. You will also have to consider security issues, as laptops are considerably more portable than desktop computers and hence are more susceptible to being stolen.

⊙ Decide whether the children will need to use a mouse or if they will be able to cope with the laptop's touch-pad or nipple to control the mouse pointer.

⊙ Make sure there is sufficient space on the children's tables for the laptop and for a mouse if one is to be used. Some laptops have quite a large 'footprint'

(the amount of desk space that they need) and may encroach on the neighbouring child's workspace, particularly if the activity requires the use of additional resources such as a notebook or a textbook.

⊙ Determine how the children will save and/or print out their work. If there is a networked printer, how do the children retrieve their work? If it is in the classroom there will be little difficulty, but if the printer is located in another part of the school, will they need to access their printouts during the lesson or at the end of the lesson? Will they save their work through the network, onto the computer's hard drive or through portable storage such as a datastick? If they save to the hard drive they will need to make a note of the computer they were using.

⊙ Plan the activity well to ensure that the use of the laptop is relevant, appropriate and productive (RAP). If the activity is relevant it should complement the subject learning and provide an opportunity for the child to apply and develop aspects of ICT capability. If it is appropriate it will make the most effective use of the ICT resource available. For example, rather than the child spending an hour laboriously typing two sentences, it might be more appropriate for him/her to be editing and improving a piece of text that had been typed in for him/her from a previously handwritten task. Finally, for the activity to be productive, the outcome should be something that has a purpose. For example, if researching the internet, the information should then be used to help the child write his/her contribution to a group booklet.

Other ICT resources

There is a tendency for ICT to be associated primarily or solely with computers. However, any form of technology that enables us to access, manipulate or present information could be deemed to be a form of ICT. This might include:

⊙ pocket computers or personal digital assistants (PDAs)

⊙ digital cameras

⊙ digital video cameras

⊙ TV and audio devices

⊙ control technology and data-logging equipment

⊙ peripheral equipment such as printers, scanners, monitors, projectors etc.

Pocket computers or PDAs

Some schools have found pocket computers to be an extremely cost-effective way of ensuring that children gain individual access to computer technology (see Learning2go at wgfl.Wolverhampton.gov.uk/pdasite). Costing about half the price of a conventional desktop computer, it is clear that more PDAs can be purchased for the same outlay. Their size and portability means that they can be easily used for activities in the classroom or on field trips. Schools that have used them extensively allow the children to take them home to complete homework tasks and also to share in the technology with their families.

PDAs are equipped with most of the usual office applications such as a word processor and spreadsheet software, and some educational software developers provide pocket PC versions of their programs. For example, the concept-mapping software, *Inspiration*, is available for use on a pocket computer. Many PDAs now include digital cameras that enable children to make notes, take pictures and even record their sounds or voice commentaries of their experiences, which can later be incorporated into multimedia presentations.

The only significant drawback to PDAs is entering text. Pocket PCs include handwriting recognition software that allows the text to be entered word by word from the screen using a stylus. It is also possible to pick letters from an on-screen keyboard, but this can prove time-consuming.

The management of PDAs is similar to that of laptops; they need to be stored and recharged, though the operating time between charges is considerably more than for a laptop. Two or three days' continuous use is quite common for PDAs. They will take up less storage space and less desk space than laptops and offer the same opportunities for wireless connection to the school network and internet – though some websites are not easy to navigate using a PDA.

The children will need to develop confidence in the use of their PDA, though it must be remembered that children tend to be more adaptable and amenable to new technologies than are the majority of adults.

Digital cameras and digital video cameras

The management of digital cameras is broadly similar, regardless of whether they take still or moving images. In fact, most cameras are capable of taking both sorts of images. As with any camera equipment, care has to be taken in their handling to prevent damage. The most significant management issues are probably those associated with transferring the images from the camera to the computer.

These days, the transfer process is usually quite straightforward. Provided the correct driver software has been installed in the computer (usually supplied on a CD with the camera), connecting the camera to the computer will almost invariably trigger the loading of the relevant program to manage the downloading of the images or camera clips. If you experience problems, refer to the manual for the camera or visit the website for the camera manufacturer, where there is often detailed advice and links to software that can be downloaded and installed.

Once the images or video clips have been transferred to the computer, editing software can be used to modify the images or to shorten, join or enhance the video clips. For more detailed guidance on making use of digital images and video for educational purposes, refer to the teacher guidance sections of the subject books (e.g. *English* project 7 – Photo-dramas; *English* project 8 – Digital video; *Humanities* project 4 – A virtual tour of a place of worship; *Science* project 8 – Digitial video – Freeze-frame, etc.).

Low-cost digital cameras provide opportunities for more children to gain hands-on experience and are less expensive to replace should they be damaged accidentally. The quality of image or video clip produced by low-cost devices is less than that produced by high-cost cameras, but they are usually sufficient for the types of activity that primary children will usually be engaged in. For the cost of one medium-priced digital camera, four low-cost cameras could be purchased. Thus a half-class set of digital cameras would cost no more than three or four full-priced alternatives.

TV and audio devices

Very few schools now make use of live TV and radio broadcasts. Programmes tend to be recorded on tape, CD or DVD for replaying at times convenient to the teacher and the timetable. Furthermore, on-line audio and video resources and the more widespread use of broadband internet links now mean that video and audio recordings can be accessed at any time to suit the needs of the curriculum.

Many classrooms are now equipped with data projectors, which are capable of projecting not only the computer screen but also the output from a video or DVD recorder. If your data projector does not include the relevant connections for these devices, it would be worthwhile asking for these to be provided. If, however, the classroom computer used with the data projector is equipped with a DVD drive, you should be able to view a DVD and play audio CDs through your computer system using Windows Media Player (Microsoft), which is usually provided as standard on all PC computers. Again, if in doubt seek technical assistance.

Control technology and data-logging equipment

Specific guidance on the use of these devices is included in the subject books (e.g. *Maths* project 1 – Using programmable toys; *Arts* project 9 – Controlling external devices; *Science* project 9 – Data logging). As indicated earlier, many of these activities are better conducted in the classroom where the other equipment and materials that are needed can be readily accessed, used and checked when, for example, a long-term data-logging experiment is under way.

Some data-logging and control devices do not need to be connected to a computer to operate. Data-loggers such as *EasySense* (Data Harvest) can be programmed to record information at set time intervals and then, once the data-collection is completed, connected to a computer for the information to be transferred. This assists greatly in the management of these activities as it does not tie up a computer for the duration of the experiment, and it enables data to be gathered from remote locations, such as an environmental area on the school field.

Peripherals

Some peripheral equipment such as printers, scanners, monitors, projectors etc. can be connected to the school's network and accessed by any computer. A centrally located colour laser printer could serve the needs of a whole school, saving on the initial cost of equipment.

The care and maintenance of peripheral equipment such as data projectors need to be handled as part of a whole-school strategy. The replacement cost for a data projector bulb can be very high, sometimes as much as half the cost of the projector itself. This needs to be budgeted for as the average life of a projector bulb is one to two years. Similarly, the running costs for printers need to be taken into account. While the life expectancy of a projector bulb cannot be extended, careful management of colour printing can lead to considerable savings over a year.

The computer suite

At first sight it might appear that managing lessons in an ICT suite is straightforward, compared to using one or two classroom computers. However, an increase in the number of computers being used at any one time inevitably increases the potential for technical problems. As explained by an experienced teacher, 'Teaching in a computer suite is like having twice the number of children to control.'

Our advice when preparing for an ICT lesson in a computer suite is:

⊙ test-run the activity on the teacher's computer

⊙ test-run the activity on one of the children's computers

⊙ test-run the activity on another computer.

Never assume that if the activity runs smoothly on your home computer it will work in the same way on the computers the children will use. For example, *Learning ICT in English* project 2 – Making talking books – requires the children to record their voices using a word processor with a record facility such as *Textease*. While this activity may run perfectly on your home computer, you might find that the children's computers have not been set up to record from a microphone. You may therefore have to check the audio control panel of every computer in the suite before the lesson to ensure that the children will be able to record their voices.

Consider how the children will be instructed and then supported while doing an activity. We suggest four approaches, though there are others:

- demonstration
- chunking
- guidance manual
- peer support.

Demonstration

Demonstration, as the name suggests, entails taking the children through a complete process before they do the activity themselves. This approach requires the children to be familiar with the software and the content for the activity and is best suited to children who are older and/or more experienced users of ICT.

Once the complete activity has been demonstrated, your role is to monitor the children's progress and intervene to support, advise or challenge.

Chunking

Chunking is similar to demonstration but a whole process or technique is broken down into a series of smaller stages or sub-tasks. The first stage is demonstrated and then the children are expected to carry it out while you monitor and support. Once they have completed one sub-task, you demonstrate the next, and so on. It is important that each sub-task includes some sort of open-ended element so that those who complete the task can elaborate on it without losing interest.

This approach is particularly suited to younger children or to when a new procedure is being introduced.

Guidance manual

A sheet or booklet is produced which guides the children through a series of routines or processes to complete an activity. The guide needs to be very carefully structured so that it can be followed independently by the children. Our experience has shown that screenshots are essential in helping to ensure that the children are supported. Some examples of guidance booklets and sheets are included on the CD-ROMs accompanying the subject books in this series. For example, see *Arts* project 7 – Using a spreadsheet model.

This approach is better suited to older children, though guidance sheets with a high proportion of screenshots can be used with younger children for relatively straightforward tasks.

Peer support

Pairing children according to ICT competence needs to be carefully managed but, if the relationships between the children are supportive, this approach can prove very beneficial. Research has shown that the success of peer support is dependent upon the extent to which the more experienced child is briefed and understands his/her role. For example, the more experienced child should not demonstrate how to do something, but should explain what to do while the less experienced child controls the mouse and the keyboard.

Another form of peer support is providing the children with 'buddies'. More experienced ICT users act as consultants who are prepared to assist others in the class who need help. Again, the children need to have a clear understanding of their roles.

Just as you should strive to encourage children to develop independence in the classroom, you should aim to help the children become less dependent on you when using the computer. Computers have an advantage over other learning resources in that they can provide users with immediate feedback on the outcomes of their actions. When typing a word into MS Word, *Textease* or *Granada Writer*, for example, the computer will immediately indicate if the word is misspelled. Children may need to be taught how to use the spell-checking features to help them correct the word. To encourage more independence in the computer suite you could set up a protocol for the children to follow when they require assistance. For example, they could be encouraged to think, 'When I have a problem I will try to fix it myself in three different ways: ask my partner; ask someone else; or ask the teacher.'

Outside the school building

From time to time, children will need to take photos, gather data or record their experiences in some way outside the classroom. In the section 'Other ICT resources', above, we explain how PDAs, digital cameras and data-loggers can be used away from the computer and the classroom. Clearly, when using electronic equipment outdoors, consideration should be paid to ensuring it does not get wet or, in the case of digital cameras, dusty. There is no risk of electrical shock from battery-operated equipment, but if a piece of equipment has been unavoidably subjected to moisture it should not be recharged or connected to computer equipment until it has had a chance to dry out thoroughly.

If equipment is to be used on a prolonged trip, such as an educational visit, it may be necessary to take spare batteries, videotapes or an additional memory card for a digital camera. Alternatively, a laptop computer, together with the necessary connection leads, could be taken along so that images or clips can be downloaded from a camera and its memory cleared for re-use.

Resources

The organisation and management of resources are critical to the success of any lesson. Although it is never possible to foresee all possible eventualities, being well organised and well prepared can help to obviate potential problems. In addition to the organisation of space, children and equipment outlined above, attention needs also to be paid to the following:

⊙ time

⊙ adult support

⊙ support materials

⊙ children's work.

Time

This is a major consideration when organising any ICT-based activity. Projects will often take more time than was originally anticipated. One of the features of ICT-based outcomes is that there is always something more that can be done. An image can have more detail added, a story can be edited, text can be inserted, words can be changed, a video can have more sound effects added to a scene, a presentation can have another animation added, more clipart can be added to a poster, and so on.

Sometimes it is necessary to insist that a piece of work is completed by a particular deadline. Some children will spend too long on peripheral details, such as changing the background colour or texture to a presentation slide, rather than working on editing the text. When chunking tasks into sub-tasks (see the section on organising activities in a computer suite earlier in this chapter), make sure the essential features, such as deciding the words to be used, are given prominence, and the peripheral aspects, such as selecting the font type, size and colour, are used as follow-ups if these are included in the learning objectives for the task.

When planning a series of lessons, leading up to a completed end-product – which is how most of the QCA scheme of work units and the projects in this series are structured – the essential elements should be planned and plotted first. Peripheral details such as those indicated above should always be added as extension tasks. You should also include time for 'finishing off' or 'enhancement' at intervals, to allow those who work more slowly to catch up.

In some of the projects in the subject books, an activity may take one or more lessons to complete. To gain some idea of the time taken to complete a project, work through the activities yourself to gain a feel for how long each activity might take, and also to determine how much support might be required and at which points. Having decided where the greatest support will be needed, you should then decide how that support should be provided – by chunking (scaffolding) the tasks, by additional adult or peer support or by the provision of support materials.

Adult support

If you are fortunate enough to have additional adult support when teaching ICT-based activities, you need to consider how best to use that support, and also the extent to which the adult needs to be briefed on the technical aspects of the software or hardware to be used. If you know the children's ICT capabilities sufficiently well to anticipate those who will need the most support and those who might need to be given additional challenge, you could differentiate your support accordingly by grouping the children. Alternatively, if using paired peer support, your adult support could be more monitorial, intervening only to facilitate, guide, assess or provide additional challenge.

There is an art – and a considerable degree of skill – involved in choosing the right moment to intervene. A feature of teachers' interventions that Ofsted has highlighted is that, with ICT, many teachers are too accepting of the children's work and do not provide sufficient challenge. Sometimes this stems from lack of confidence with the software, which is why it is important to work through ICT-based activities before teaching them to children.

Our advice about intervention is to assume that the child can improve on what he/she has done – the skill comes in choosing the appropriate level of challenge to suit the child concerned. We suggest some of the following as possible responses.

Assuming you have provided some positive feedback on the work produced, you could follow up with:

- 'Have you tried: using a different font/seeing what happens if . . ./changing the colour (or size or style) of . . . ?'

- 'Have you seen: this technique/that tool/what happens when . . . ?'

- 'I wonder if you could: make that part stand out more/make that clearer/ make that sentence even more scary?'

- 'What do you think would happen if: you changed the size of that word/you changed the background colour/you made that heading stand out more?'

- 'Watch what happens if I: change this/add that/move those.'

The great advantage of computer-based activities is that, provided an earlier version has been saved, if a modification doesn't work, the original version can be recovered. Because ICT enables experimentation, you as a teacher should encourage the children to keep trying things out. Adopt the 'What if?' approach.

Support materials

Support materials can take the form of:

- guidance sheets or booklets

- prompt sheets

- on-screen help

- video tutorials

- interactive tutorials

- wall charts and posters.

Guidance sheets or booklets

These are sometimes provided with the software or can be produced by you to meet the needs of the children you are teaching. Some examples are provided on the CD-ROMs that accompany the subject books in this series.

Prompt sheets

These can take the form of handouts or worksheets that the children use or complete either by hand or on screen as they progress through a project or activity.

For example, when using the database to solve the crimes in the Villains activity (*English* project 5), the children will find a print-out of the crime stories useful. Some software companies provide activity sheets for their programs. For example, Valiant provides a set of work cards for children, setting out activities for the *Roamer* floor robot. All prompt sheets for the activities in the projects in this series are provided on the CD-ROMs accompanying each subject book.

On-screen help

Many programs include comprehensive on-screen help for the user. For example, all Microsoft Office programs include a Help menu. Some educational software, such as *Imagine LOGO*, *Textease* and *Granada Toolkit* include help screens designed for use by children. Children should be taught how, and encouraged, to make use of these facilities to help them become more autonomous and independent. In the plenary for each ICT lesson you could ask particular children to demonstrate a new technique or routine they have discovered by working through some of the help screens.

Video tutorials

Some programs, most notably those provided by 2Simple, include video tutorials that demonstrate procedures and routines through the use of on-screen videos with commentaries. Provided the content is appropriate to the project or activity that the children were engaged in, these could be used to provide the children with the next 'chunk' of information.

Some on-screen video tutorials are provided on the CD-ROM accompanying *Learning ICT with English*, demonstrating how *Sound Recorder* works (project 4 – Working with audio).

Interactive tutorials

Unlike a video tutorial, over which the viewer has little control, other than to stop or start it, an interactive tutorial makes use of the multimedia capabilities of a computer as it guides the user through a series of tasks. Interactive tutorials can be purchased for all the Microsoft Office applications but are aimed primarily at adults. These can be useful should you wish to learn about some of the more advanced features of the software on your computer. Many websites provide on-line interactive tutorials on familiar software such as *PowerPoint*. Again, these are mostly intended for adults.

Occasionally, you might want to use interactive tutorials with some of the more advanced children at key stage 2 who need an extra level of challenge, one that you feel unable to provide, either because of time constraints or the limitations of your own expertise.

Wall charts and posters

Some educational programs include posters reminding the children of the program's key features or providing contexts for activities. For example, *Number Magic* (RM) is supplied with a poster showing the basic features of the program, and a series of Barnaby Bear resources includes posters designed to encourage interest and involvement by the children (see *Humanities* project 1 – Decision making with a mouse).

More general posters related to primary school ICT can be obtained from suppliers such as DayDream Education (www.daydreameducation.co.uk) and AVP (avp.100megs28.com).

You can also make your own posters and wallcharts, of course. *Textease* includes a facility for creating posters and banners of any size using a standard A4 printer.

Children's work

Systems for enabling children to save and retrieve their work are outlined in the section 'The classroom computer', above. It is assumed that if the school has a computer suite then a system will have been devised for ensuring that the teachers, classes and individual children have designated network space to save their files. This section examines what children will do with their completed ICT activities.

If ICT activities are properly embedded in subject-related contexts, then the outcomes should be included in the children's workbooks or displays related to the relevant subject(s). Occasionally, the outcomes will be whole-class efforts, such as a class story, an information booklet or a display to which several groups have contributed. It may be possible to create several copies of the final product so that each group, or even each child, has its own.

Some ICT-based activities will produce outcomes that are not paper-based – for example, video films or computer-based presentations. If you want the children to produce a hard copy of their work, it is often possible to print out presentations. *PowerPoint* (Microsoft), for example, includes a feature that enables you to print handouts with up to nine thumbnail images of each slide on an A4 sheet. Taking screenshots of videos is sometimes not very straightforward. *Media Player* (Microsoft), for example, does not include a facility for taking freeze-frame shots of videos. *Moviemaker*, free with Windows XP, does have a snapshot tool, as does the *Digital Blue Movie Creator* software described in *Arts* project 10. Alternatively, if you would like the children to include 'stills' from their digital video productions a piece of freeware called *Imexor* (*WackyCoder*) is available as a download from (www.wackycoder.com). The saved images could be inserted into a paper-based storyboard, for example, showing the key scenes in the children's production.

Summary

In this chapter we have focused on how ICT resources and equipment can be organised and managed in the primary school. A classroom-based computer can provide opportunities for ICT to be embedded more fully into subject learning and teaching and for children to learn how ICT tools can assist them with other learning tasks such as accessing information, consulting reference resources such as dictionaries and encyclopaedias, or checking calculations. Through careful management, it is suggested that one or two classroom computers can provide children with hands-on experience on a weekly basis.

The management of ICT activities in a computer suite needs to be carefully planned to ensure that children are not all clamouring for support or attention at the same time. Some management strategies are suggested for introducing new procedures and techniques with emphasis placed on ensuring that core outcomes are achieved, and peripheral details, such as the appearance of a page, are used as extension activities.

Laptop computers provide a useful compromise between classroom-based computers and the computer suite. They can be used to augment classroom work as the need arises. The greatest limitation is battery life between recharges. This needs to be taken into account when planning and preparing activities using laptop computers.

The key issue arising from this chapter is that successful ICT activities require careful preparation and double-checking on the computers the children will use before it can be assumed that any activity will work. The most important piece of advice we can give to anyone planning to use ICT with children is that if it can go wrong, it will go wrong. The secret of success is cutting down the opportunities for error by rehearsing each activity, and then rehearsing it again.

CHAPTER 6

The future

Several pathways through curriculum subjects have been described in this series. The progression charts in Chapter 2 are designed to help with the creation of long-term plans that can help you and your colleagues address the development of ICT capability with your children in contexts that play to your strengths. We have rooted all the projects in contexts that are designed to support the subject learning and interest and inspire the children using currently available technologies. While advances will be made in the technology, the principles described at the start of this book, advocating the integration of ICT tasks for the benefit of ICT capability and subject learning alike, will hold good.

The late Douglas Adams, author of *The Hitchhiker's Guide to the Galaxy*, came up with a set of rules that describe and explain our responses to new technologies:

1. Anything that is in the world when you're born is normal and ordinary and is just a natural part of the way the world works.

2. Anything that's invented between when you're fifteen and thirty-five is new and exciting and revolutionary and you can probably get a career in it.

3. Anything invented after you're thirty-five is against the natural order of things.

Adams (2002: 95)

It is worth our while reflecting on the fact that those ICTs that motivate and inspire us will not necessarily have the same effect on the children we teach, and vice versa. Very few technologies have initially been developed with education in mind. The micro-electronics industry that gave rise to personal computers was developed for military purposes. The internet was, in part, born out of Cold War paranoia, and much of the software described in the projects in this series has its roots in office tasks. The real developments that have taken and will take place in education are in the ways that new technologies are used.

So what might be around the corner and how will it impact on primary education?

With some degree of certainty we can predict that developments will occur in:

⊙ hardware and software

⊙ networking

⊙ pedagogy

⊙ school buildings and classrooms.

Terms such as e-pedagogy, e-learning, e-teaching, e-reading, e-writing etc. abound, but what do they mean? This final chapter considers some possible futures in each of these areas.

Hardware and software

The tendency over recent years has been the reduction in size and cost of ICT devices, coupled with an increase in the range of functions that are available. As we discussed in the previous chapter, there are already several schools that are providing children with personal digital assistants (PDAs) or palmtop computers (Perry 2003). These small, handheld devices can perform most of the functions that you would expect of a computer. If the density of transistors on a computer chip continues to double every 18 months, increasing the performance of computers, it is predicted that by around 2020 there will be supercomputers with the capacity, if not the capability, of a human mind, and that 2035 would see microcomputers with this kind of capability. What that will mean for education we just cannot say.

Others suggest a trend toward computers becoming concealed within appliances. ICT in education would then evolve into learning to use these intelligent appliances to undertake tasks and solve problems. In the same way that knowledge and understanding of programming and computer architecture has been made redundant through the development of operating systems, it is possible that some of the skills, routines and techniques described in this series will be performed automatically by these new appliances.

The familiar graphical user interface (GUI), which saw the advent of the mouse and now other pointing devices to operate computer applications via menus and icons, will not last for ever. *Google Earth* (freely downloadable from the Google website), which provides a visual interface enabling easy access to vast amounts of geographical data and satellite photographs, has made a huge leap forward. It has been possible for some time to use voice and wearable items, such as virtual reality gloves, which enable the wearer's actions to be recognised by the software. It is possible that another revolution in the human machine interface will see these technologies being used routinely to operate technology.

One of the greatest changes in ICT use in schools has been brought about by the introduction of electronic whiteboards (EWs) – the 'interactive' has been omitted on purpose as the technology is not, of itself, interactive. Some have argued that part of the reason for the swift adoption of EW technology is the ease with which the boards can support traditional 'interpassive' teaching methods; others delude themselves that 30 or so children are all able to use one computer simultaneously. Used effectively, there is some evidence that pedagogy (see below) is beginning to evolve in response to their use. Several other interactive devices are already being used with EWs in classrooms. Wireless tablets can enable interaction from around the classroom, and some wireless voting devices enable children to contribute answers, views and opinions via wireless handsets to display instant responses on the screen. The traditional EW and projector arrangement is being questioned, however. Some find the 'shadowless' plasma screen more effective and some research has been carried out with boards placed at a 30-degree angle to help young learners interact more easily. Recently, a 'FogScreen' has been developed that enables images to be projected in the air on a dry fog, which can be touched to emulate mouse operation and 'walked through'! Beware, Alice!

A huge potential for education using the internet has been released through the development of WIKI (actually derived from a Hawaiian word meaning quick but sometimes contrived to stand for 'What I Know Is'). WIKI refers to web pages that can be edited so that knowledge can be added. Several Wikipaedias – evolving encyclopaedias – are available on the web (for example, sco.widipedia.org/wiki), developing and recording local and regional knowledge.

Networking

Many schools have installed wireless networks that enable access to files and the internet anywhere in the building. Indeed, there are many locations within cities and motorway services in the UK where the internet can be accessed wirelessly by wireless-enabled computers and PDAs. The locus of educational computing has shifted from stand-alone classroom computers to networked computer suites to wireless-enabled laptops and portable devices that can respond to the most appropriate organisation for the planned learning.

The bandwidth of connectivity is currently doubling approximately every six months, enabling greater use of mobile telephony and computing devices. The UK government has aspirations to enable all children to have personal access to their work and learning resources any time, anywhere.

E-pedagogy

It has been claimed that, as we continue to use ICT in education and become more familiar and confident in its use, new methods of teaching and learning will inevitably evolve (John and Sutherland 2004). But will they? *Is* it inevitable? Will ICT make huge improvements to education as measured by children's performance? The research is not as conclusive as ICT enthusiasts would wish. Some projects that identify measurable differences in children's performance during the life of the project have not seen the benefits sustained once the project is over (Higgins *et al.* 2005). Others have described significant changes in teachers' practice, particularly with respect to EW use (Smith 2002).

A Luddite perspective could suggest that computers will make teachers redundant in the same way that advances in textile technology made textile workers redundant in the nineteenth century. There is no doubt that some computer-based learning can be very effective, and we will get better at designing learning programs. Some currently available on-line adventure games, however, are not vastly different in approach from Anita Straker's text-based adventures designed for BBC computers over 20 years ago. By embracing what the technology requires, in terms of skills and understanding, and what it affords, in terms of learning opportunities, the role and skills of effective teachers will evolve.

It has been recognised by education authorities around the world (tardily in some cases) that technology without continuing professional development (CPD) and pre-service training for teachers is wasteful of the resource. As the technology and the pedagogy evolve, continued investment in training for teachers will be needed.

What form will training need to take?

There needs to be additional emphasis on evaluating sources and on library research skills. ICT has led to what some call a Global Digital Library and we are able to access seemingly limitless amounts of information from vast databases. The huge success of Google and its controversial intention to make large numbers of books available digitally means that teachers will need to be able to help children access and evaluate information. It will be more important than ever to engage in genuine enquiry with young learners, helping to devise and answer their own questions, and not solely to discover predetermined facts from a finite number of sources. Resources like *Google Earth*, which enables virtual exploration of our planet through a novel interface, will turn children into empowered explorers.

Whether or not teachers seek to develop children's ability to use ICT, it has become a part of nearly all subject disciplines and contributes, in part, to the overcrowding of the curriculum discussed earlier in this book. Subject teachers will continue to need growing amounts of subject-related ICT knowledge for teaching with and about the tools that apply to the subject, like spreadsheets, geographical information systems, databases, image-editing and design tools. For primary teachers, that knowledge could be immense.

Some researchers have already identified that children are developing ways of learning based on risk-taking and trial and improvement, ways that are learned from exposure to computer games and other technologies. Models of school learning that do not respond to this development are going to risk exacerbating a growing mismatch between school learning and life in the eyes of some young learners. That is not to say that new models of teaching and learning are going to be created solely by the learners; using knowledge of how children learn, we will need to evaluate ways in which new and emerging technologies can be used to good effect.

There are already plenty of publishing opportunities on-line – formal (moderated or reviewed websites), and informal (discussion boards, blogs [web logs], some types of on-line chat). We will learn, as they lose their novelty, to evaluate and assess the quality of these types of e-writing and the learning they evidence. The tools that ICT-based writing affords can be put to good effect to enhance the quality of communication. It has been suggested that contributions to e-mail or on-line discussions could even form the basis of assessments in the future.

The Department for Education and Skills, in *Fulfilling the Potential: Transforming Teaching and Learning through ICT in Schools* (DfES 2003), describes several case studies in which a child of the future submits homework, receives feedback on work completed and asks questions of the teacher – all on-line via a personal log-in space on the internet. The child works independently or collaboratively with classmates, from home or at school, and is always able to access learning resources from any computer with an internet connection. Most of the approaches to learning outlined in the document are already happening and will be recognised as reality by some children. Some of the consequences for teachers are also being realised, but transforming teaching and learning for all children will have a dramatic impact on the role of the teacher as we become cast as advisers and managers of children's learning using technology.

School buildings and classrooms

In 1985, Apple undertook a research-and-development collaboration among public schools, universities and research agencies. It aimed to study how routine use of technology by teachers and students might change teaching and learning. It was entitled Apple Classrooms of Tomorrow (ACOT). The ACOT research project came to an end in 1998 after 13 years of equipping classrooms to be technology-rich learning environments. Much of what was learned related to educational change and how new technologies, curricula and new ideas about learning and teaching need to develop side-by-side.

In 2002, Estelle Morris, the then Secretary of State for Education, announced 'Classrooms of the future becoming a reality'. Since then an ambitious building programme has been undertaken. Innovative designs of buildings that incorporate 'cybercafés' and support individualised learning have been undertaken. A dozen local authorities in the UK have been supported to pilot new and innovative ideas for the design of educational settings. Following the remodelling of the education workforce that has been undertaken, a further initiative called Teaching Environments for the Future (TEF) has set out to consider how new ways of working, brought about by the remodelling agenda, can be supported by remodelling buildings and learning environments.

Many schools have experimented with the organisation and layout of ICT since its introduction in the 1980s. Probably the biggest impact has been on libraries and resource areas. Many of us have witnessed the move from classroom computer to computer suite to mobile wireless laptops, used in sets or individually in classrooms and in the wider school environment. In truth, any layout has its advantages and disadvantages. Many teachers have found that the promise of mobile computing has been limited by the life of batteries and the management of recharging. The whiteboard in every classroom is fast becoming a reality in the UK, however, and with it the return of a classroom computer that enables additional flexibility. As the technology becomes smaller, lighter and wireless, the demands it places upon the physical layout of the school will reduce.

Some argue that with current levels of truancy we are actually educating a smaller percentage of the nation's children than in the Gradgrind institutions of the nineteenth century. Several experiments exploring radical arrangements for education in the future have been carried out with pupils described as 'school-phobic', to keep them learning. One research project called NotSchool, run by Ultralab, has developed an on-line virtual school environment for children who could not cope with the traditional school community. The project has proved itself in trials and has been rolled out to several local authorities in the UK

(Millwood 2006). Could it become a future alternative for all children, enabling access to learning without attending school at all?

SCHOME is another research project that uses ICT to meld school and home learning. It sets out to explore and draw together ideas for an education system for the information age. Ideas such as a 'one-room schoolhouse' (Marcus 1997), equipped with technology but with no walls or classes or timetable, have been explored in the US. As technology opens up possibilities, we will be forced to consider what the important essential ingredients are for the education of twenty-first-century children, as some of the experiences and social interactions that we have taken for granted, as a fortuitous bonus to mass education, could disappear.

Summary

However meteoric developments in technology may seem to be, human evolution takes place at an altogether slower rate. We will have to learn about new technological developments frequently and possibly quickly. By maintaining a clear perspective on learning and how children learn, we will be able to evaluate the contributions that new and evolving technologies can make to education.

The questions below will help assess any new developments:

⊙ To which areas of learning does the technology contribute?

⊙ How difficult is it to use?

⊙ Will learning to use it be useful in itself or solely a means to an end?

⊙ Will using it avoid other learning or make it redundant?

⊙ Is it useful for all learners or only for some?

References and further reading

Adams, D. (2002) *The Salmon of Doubt.* London: PanMacmillan.

Buckingham, D., Sefton-Green, J. and Willett, R. (2003) *Shared Spaces: Informal Learning and Digital Cultures.* Centre for the Study of Children, Youth and Media. Institute of Education, University of London. Accessed April 2006 (http://wac.co.uk/sharedspaces/final_report.pdf).

DfES (2003) *Fulfilling the Potential: Transforming Teaching and Learning through ICT in Schools.* London: DfES (http://www.teachernet.gov.uk/_doc/4382/ICTiS%20directions.doc – accessed March 2006).

Higgins, S., Falzon, C. and Hall, I. *et al.* (2005) *Embedding ICT in the Literacy and Numeracy Strategies.* Final Report (www.becta.org.uk/page_documents/research/univ_newcastle_evaluation_whiteboards.pdf – accessed March 2006). Institute of Education, University of London (2006) (http://wac.co.uk/sharedspaces/research.php – accessed March 2006).

John, P. and Sutherland, R. (2004) 'Teaching and learning with ICT: new technology, new pedagogy?' *Education, Communication & Information*, 4(1), March.

Marcus, J. (1997) 'One-room schoolhouse keys into the future'. *Times Educational Supplement*, 31 October (http://www.tes.co.uk/search/story/?story_id=156021 – accessed 31 March 2006).

Millwood (2006) Notschool.Net Project (http://ww3.ultralab.net/projects/notschool/projectdescription/?searchterm=None – accessed 2 April 2006).

Moursund, D. G. (2004) *Planning, Forecasting and Inventing Your Computers-in-Education Future* (http://darkwing.uoregon.edu/~moursund/InventingFutures/index.htm – accessed March 2006).

Parrott, M. (n.d.) *Towards a New Literacy.* Cambridge International Examinations (http://www.cie.org.uk/CIE/WebSite/ICT/article1.jsp – accessed March 2006).

Perry, D. (2003) *Handheld Computers (PDAs) in Schools.* Report. London: Becta/DfES.

Sefton-Green, J. and Willett, R. (2003). 'Living and learning in chatrooms (or does informal learning have anything to teach us?)' *Éducation et Sociétiés*, vol. 2. English version available on-line (http://wac.co.uk/sharedspaces/research.php – accessed April 2006).

Smith, A. (2002) *Interactive Whiteboard Evaluation* (www.mirandanet.ac.uk – accessed March 2006).

Learning objectives for each project covered by the subject books

Learning ICT in the Arts

Project number	Project name	Learning objective	Aspects of ICT capability
1	Building places	Drag items on screen	Skills and routines
		Select and use tools to make different marks on the page	Skills and routines
		ICT is used in a variety of ways in the world around them	Key ideas
		Ideas and thoughts can be communicated by using ICT tools	Key ideas
		ICT in learning is enjoyable and can be an interactive experience	Key ideas
2	Aboriginal art	Arrange and re-arrange graphic objects on a page to create art work	Techniques
		Images can be created by combining and manipulating objects	Techniques
		Information can be presented in a variety of forms and collected from a variety of sources	Key ideas
		Artwork is provisional until printed	Key ideas
3	Designing an environment	Select, move, rotate and resize graphic objects	Skills and routines
		Images can be created by combining and manipulating objects	Skills and routines
		Pictures can provide information and computers can represent real situations	Key ideas

Project number	Project name	Learning objective	Aspects of ICT capability
		A computer representation allows you to make choices, explore alternatives and evaluate different outcomes	Key ideas
4	Designing logos	Copy and paste parts of a 'painting'	Skills and routines
		Pictures can be assembled by repeating elements	Techniques
		Change colours and evaluate choices	Techniques
		Making marks on the screen using 'undo' makes it easy to correct mistakes and explore alternatives	Techniques
		A screen image can be a finished product	Key ideas
		Images can be created by combining and manipulating objects	Key ideas
5	Digital photos	Pictures can be assembled by repeating elements	Skills and routines
		Images can be created by combining and manipulating photographs	Techniques
		Select and use different techniques to communicate ideas through pictures	Techniques
		Images can be recorded, stored and transferred digitally	Key ideas
		Computer software can include a range of media which gives the user options to explore	Key ideas
6	Sound pictures	Select skills and techniques to organise, reorganise and communicate ideas	Techniques
		Electronic and live sounds can be combined in a performance	Techniques
		ICT can be used to record and manipulate sounds to develop and refine a musical composition	Key ideas
		Sounds can be stored as computer files	Key ideas
7	Using a spreadsheet model	Select a cell and add information to a spreadsheet	Skills and routines
		Explore the effect of changing the variables in a model and use them to make and test predictions	Techniques
		Computer models enable alternatives to be explored and decisions to be evaluated	Key ideas
		Organising information can help to answer questions	Key ideas
8	LOGO animation	Create and control multiple turtle shapes	Skills and routines
		Write repeating procedures to produce a desired outcome	Skills and routines

Project number	Project name	Learning objective	Aspects of ICT capability
		LOGO procedures can call other procedures	Techniques
		ICT makes it easy to explore alternatives	Key ideas
		ICT can be used to develop images	Key ideas
9	Controlling external devices	Write repeating procedures to produce a desired outcome	Techniques
		Machines and devices are controlled and control devices must be programmed	Key ideas
		Sequence affects outcome	Key ideas
		Instructions can be recorded for replication and amendment	Key ideas
		Recording a sequence of instructions forms the basis of control work	Key ideas
10	Creating a digital 'silent film'	Select suitable information and media and prepare it for processing using ICT	Techniques
		Organise, refine and present information in different forms for a specific audience	Techniques
		ICT makes it easy to arrange and reorder video clips and explore alternatives	Key ideas
		ICT can be used to develop images and a screen image can be a finished product	Key ideas
		Pictures and sounds can be combined in a performance	Key ideas

Learning ICT with English

Project number	Project name	Learning objective	Aspects of ICT capability
1	Using talking book	Interact with text, images and animations through use of the mouse	Skills and routines
		Associate text with words and sounds	Techniques
		Computers can store and present information as text, pictures, sounds and moving images	Key ideas
2	Making talking books	Enter text, images and sounds into a computer	Techniques
		Computer-based talking stories are written by authors and not computers	Key ideas
		Evaluate a piece of work completed on a computer and suggest improvements	Key ideas
		Computers can be used to manipulate text, images and sounds	Key ideas

Project number	Project name	Learning objective	Aspects of ICT capability
8	Making an information source	Insert images and sounds into a multimedia authoring program	Skills and routines
		Search for images and sounds on the web using simple and more complex search strategies	Techniques
		Use a multimedia authoring program to refine and present information in different forms for a specific audience	Techniques
		Compare the presentation of information with multimedia to presentation by paper-based means	Key ideas
9	A video of a visit to a place of worship	Assemble a short digital video using still images, audio and text	Techniques
		Digital video can be used to convey an impression of a place of worship, focusing on its character and symbolism	Key ideas

Learning ICT with Mathematics

Project number	Project name	Learning objective	Aspects of ICT capability
1	Using programmable toys	Small forward moves can be combined, i.e. the basis of addition	Skills and routines
		Backward moves negate forward moves, i.e. the basis of subtraction	Skills and routines
		Programmable toys can be given instructions which they remember and can be changed	Key ideas
2	Counting	Communicate information about the size and differences between sets of objects	Techniques
		Objects can be represented by images, icons or blocks and despite the representation the same information can be deduced	Key ideas
		Objects can be classified and sorted into sets	Key ideas
3	Shopping	Interpret amounts of money displayed on screen	Skills and routines
		Relate real objects to images on screen	Skills and routines
		Supermarket tills are a form of computer	Key ideas
4	Exploring with directions	The foundations of LOGO turtle graphics programming	Techniques
		Regular shapes can be drawn using a repeated series of the same instructions	Key ideas

Project number	Project name	Learning objective	Aspects of ICT capability
		LOGO procedures comprise a series of instructions which can be amended	Key ideas
5	Symmetry and tessellation	Design tessellating shapes using a paint program or a tessellation or tiling program	Skills and routines
		Use a drawing program or tools to explore symmetry and tessellation	Techniques
6	Statistical investigations 1	Search for records which meet particular criteria in a database	Skills and routines
		Present information as bar charts in a database	Skills and routines
		To create a simple database	Skills and routines
		Transfer a chart/graph as an image from a database to a word-processed document	Skills and routines
7	LOGO challenges	Control a screen turtle	Skills and routines
		Write and use LOGO procedures	Skills and routines
		Apply knowledge of LOGO to solve given and self-created challenges and problems	Techniques
8	Modelling investigations	Create and use a spreadsheet model	Skills and routines
		Explore simulations systematically	Techniques
		Use a spreadsheet to investigate	Techniques
		Simulations enable people to investigate 'What if . . . ?' situations	Key ideas
9	Patterns and spreadsheets	Enter formulae into spreadsheets	Skills and routines
		Use spreadsheets to investigate functions and number patterns	Techniques
		Spreadsheets can be used to explore the interrelationships between number operations	Key ideas
10	Statistical investigations 2	Interpret scattergraphs	Skills and routines
		Use a database or spreadsheet to analyse data	Techniques
		Form and test hypotheses	Techniques
		Conduct a statistical investigation using a database or spreadsheet	Techniques
		To use a database or spreadsheet to analyse data	Key ideas

Learning ICT with Science

Project data	Project name	Learning objective	Aspects of ICT capability
1	Drag and drop sorting	Objects can be described, identified and sorted using keywords	Techniques
		Object-based drawing software can be used to model and present sorting activities	Techniques
		Pictures provide information	Key ideas
		ICT can help to sort and present information	Key ideas
		ICT can be used to communicate ideas through pictures	Key ideas
		ICT makes it easy to correct mistakes and explore alternatives	Key ideas
2	Digital microscope – time-lapse	Use ICT to test a hypothesis	Techniques
		Control devices must be programmed	Techniques
		Use ICT appropriately to communicate ideas through text and images	Techniques
		Information can be collected from pictures and can be presented in a variety of forms	Key ideas
		Devices that carry out repeated actions follow stored instructions which can include numbers	Key ideas
		Computers can represent real situations	Key ideas
3	Concept cartoons	Computers use icons to provide information and instructions	Key ideas
		ICT can be used to create pictures to present information	Key ideas
		ICT makes it easy to correct mistakes and explore alternatives	Key ideas
4	Branching databases	Prepare data for a database, with an awareness that some questions have only yes/no answers and have to be phrased carefully	Techniques
		A tree diagram can be used to organise information and a branching database can be used to store and sort information which can be searched	Key ideas
		A database can only answer questions if appropriate data have been entered	Key ideas
		Objects can be divided according to criteria and collecting and storing information in an organised way helps them find answers to questions	Key ideas
5	Graphical representation of data	Enter data in a spreadsheet and present findings	Techniques
		Identify and correct implausible and inaccurate data	Techniques

Project data	Project name	Learning objective	Aspects of ICT capability
		Information comes from a variety of sources and can be presented in a variety of forms	Key ideas
		ICT can be used for collecting, storing and sorting information in an organised way	Key ideas
		Data represented graphically can be easier to understand than textual data	Key ideas
6	Giant's hand	Interpret and analyse information in graphs	Skills and routines
		Identify and correct implausible and inaccurate data	Techniques
		Use ICT to classify information and present findings	Techniques
		Use straightforward lines of enquiry	Techniques
		Work with others to interpret information	Techniques
		ICT can be used for collecting, storing and sorting information in an organised way	Key ideas
		Data represented graphically can be easier to understand than textual data	Key ideas
		Information can be represented as graphs but this can only provide limited answers to questions	Key ideas
		Lines of best fit can suggest patterns and relationships between measurements	Key ideas
7	Multimedia information source	Use ICT appropriately to communicate ideas through text	Skills and routines
		Select suitable information and media and prepare it for processing using ICT	Techniques
		Select and use different techniques to communicate ideas through pictures	Techniques
		Use a multimedia authoring program to organise, refine and present information in different forms for a specific audience	Techniques
		Information comes from a variety of sources and can be presented in a variety of forms	Key ideas
		Computers use icons to provide information and instructions	Key ideas
		Use ICT to organise, reorganise and analyse ideas and information	Key ideas
		A screen image can be a finished product	Key ideas
8	Digital video – freeze-frame	Record and edit video and view a frame at a time	Skills and routines
		Form and test hypotheses	Techniques

Project data	Project name	Learning objective	Aspects of ICT capability
		Information comes from a variety of sources and can be presented in a variety of forms	Key ideas
		Video can be used to identify patterns and relationships	Key ideas
		Video can be used to monitor changes in environmental conditions	Key ideas
		A video can be used to can-take samples of data for a set period of time	Key ideas
9	Data-logging	Interpret and analyse information in graphs	Skills and routines
		Form and test hypotheses	Techniques
		Line graphs can be used to show continuously changing information	Techniques
		Identify opportunities and design simple investigations for which the collection of data through a computer device is both feasible and advantageous	Techniques
		Information comes from a variety of sources and can be presented in a variety of forms	Key ideas
		ICT can be used to store and sort information	Key ideas
		Data represented graphically can be easier to understand than textual data	Key ideas
		Information can be represented as graphs but this can only provide limited answers to questions	Key ideas
		Sensing devices can be used to monitor changes in environmental conditions	Key ideas
		A computer can take samples of data for a set period of time	Key ideas
10	Using search engines	Use the tools in on-line search engines to find out the answers to specific questions	Skills and routines
		Use complex searches to locate information	Techniques
		Information comes from a variety of sources and can be presented in a variety of forms	Key ideas
		Information can be connected in different ways at the same time	Key ideas
		Searches can be carried out using more than one criterion	Key ideas
		Understand the importance of choosing key words to find information	Key ideas

Index